STAN TOLER'S PRACTICAL GUIDE FOR PASTORAL MINISTRY

STAN TOLER

wesleyan
publishing
house

Indianapolis, Indiana

Copyright © 2007 by Wesleyan Publishing House
Published by Wesleyan Publishing House
Indianapolis, Indiana 46250
Printed in the United States of America

Library of Congress Cataloging-in-Publication Data

Toler, Stan.
   Stan Toler's practical guide for pastoral ministry / Stan Toler.
   p. cm.
   ISBN-13: 978-0-89827-353-3
   ISBN-10: 0-89827-353-6
   1. Pastoral theology. I. Title. II. Title: Practical guide for
pastoral ministry.
   BV4011.3.T64 2006
   253--dc22
                                        2006036073

To my wife, Linda, and sons, Seth and Adam—

Thanks for taking this incredible journey with me
Your love, support, and encouragement has made all the
difference in my thirty years of pastoral ministry

CONTENTS

Preface   9

Acknowledgments   11

PART 1: PERSONAL GROWTH   13

1. Characteristics of Great Pastors   15
2. Discovering Joy in Ministry   19
3. Reflecting the Holiness of God   22
4. Keys to Flawless Character   25
5. Steps to Pastoral Health   29
6. Creating a Dynamic Devotional Life   33
7. Facing Personal Attacks   37
8. Pastoring the Pastor   41
9. Powering Up for Ministry   44
10. Making a Good Impression   47
11. Surviving Change   51
12. Thriving amid Adversity   55
13. Improving Your Integrity   59
14. How to Get Time Off   63

PART 2: FAMILY LIFE   67

15. Making Your House a Home   69
16. How to Get Along with Anybody   73
17. Marks of a Healthy Family   76
18. Financial Habits for Life   80
19. Bringing Out the Best in Your Family   84
20. How to Make Others Feel Important   88
21. Creating an Atmosphere of Affirmation   91
22. Power Listening   95
23. Say Good-bye to Bitterness   98

PART 3: MINISTRY 102

24. Delivering Consistent Pastoral Care 103
25. Adding Doors to Your Church 107
26. Conducting the Funeral 111
27. Conducting the Wedding 115
28. Planning the Worship Service 119
29. Extending Your Influence 123
30. Ensuring a Second Visit 126
31. Leading a Worship Team 131
32. Inspiring Confidence 135
33. Effective Evangelism 139
34. Improving Your Print Image 143
35. Ten Tips for Hospital Visitation 147
36. Reviving a Lukewarm Church 151
37. How to Offer Correction 155
38. What to Do When Members Leave 159
39. Recruiting Top Volunteers 163

PART 4: LEADERSHIP 167

40. The Prerequisite for Church Leadership 169
41. Five Marks of a Great Leader 173
42. Casting Faith-Inspired Vision 177
43. Building a Winning Team 180
44. Directing Attention 184
45. Evaluating Opportunities 187
46. How to Recruit Leaders 190
47. Tips for Training Leaders 193
48. Seven Teams You Need 196
49. Ensuring Institutional Integrity 200
50. Five Ways to Expand Your Expertise 203
51. Becoming a Spiritual Leader 207
52. Leading Under Authority 211
53. Managing Change 215
54. Managing Risk 219
55. Leading in Uncertain Times 222

PART 5: COACHING 225

56. Enlisting Others to Achieve the Vision 226
57. Inspiring Others to Succeed 229
58. Becoming a Leader Who Inspires Confidence 232
59. Orchestrating the Work of Others 236
60. Qualities of a Mentor 240
61. Taking Responsibility for Your Ministry 244
62. Team-Building Tips 247
63. Defining Success in Ministry 251
64. Inspiring Others to Dream 254
65. Inspiring Others to Follow 257

PART 6: COMMUNICATION 261

66. Essential Preaching Skills 262
67. Preaching for Life Change 266
68. Earning an Audience's Attention 270
69. How to Get Your Message Across 274
70. Using Story in Preaching 278
71. Using Humor Effectively 282
72. How to Talk about Money 286
73. Communicating Your Vision in Writing 290
74. Keys to a Successful Board Meeting 294
75. Staying on the Cutting Edge 298

Afterword 303

PREFACE

If you are interested in being the best pastor you can be and in leading people to a new level of excellence in their journey with Christ, this book is for you. This is a book about becoming a vibrant, passionate, effective ministry leader. It's about winning championships, not playing games. These pages represent a distillation of the many lessons I've learned out there on the field in the heat of the competition.

I'm often told that I have a pastor's heart. If that means that I have a heart for local church ministry, then it's true. I've been a pastor more than thirty years in small, midsize, and larger churches. If it means that my heart is with pastors and Christian leaders, that is true also. Years ago someone took the time to mentor me—to teach me about working with people, about leadership principles, and about teaching and preaching the truth of God's Word. I'm still learning.

I'm also learning how to teach others. Being in front of a class or auditorium teaching other pastors and their staff members how to do vibrant ministry is one of my favorite pursuits; and I've been doing it for at least twenty-five years. In seminars, conferences, and international speaking engagements, I have had the honor of meeting dedicated Christian leaders—people like you—servants of Christ who have experienced the joys and challenges of leading others while still hungering to learn more about ministry. Twenty-first-century leadership is a construction zone. We are always working to sharpen our skills so that we can motivate others to be their best for God.

In this book, I'm sharing a portion of what I've learned over the years. Much of that learning took place in classrooms, libraries, and conferences, but most of it was acquired in the only setting that really matters—on the job in worship centers, auditoriums, fellowship buildings, classrooms, and boardrooms. I've been where you are, and I'm still there. I know what it's like to bear the responsibility for raising funds for a building project that seems just out of reach. I've felt the boardroom stares from folk who would rather have shown me the highway than do things a different way. And I've stood beside grieving loved ones, praying that the Holy Spirit would offer some word through me that might comfort them in their pain. I know the challenges of pastoral ministry, and I pray that these chapters will be a help to you. I pray that they will motivate you, enlarge your vision, rekindle your passion, and provide the practical help that you need for doing ministry in these changing times.

You'll find resources here for dealing with almost every area of ministry. In my seminars, I often make the statement "It's not about theory, it's about practice." That accurately describes my approach to pastoral ministry—and the contents of this book. Principles are explained, but most important are the practical tips you'll need to grow personally and to help you grow your church or organization.

I'm on your team! We are laborers together in the great work of the Kingdom. Let us be satisfied with nothing less than excellence.

Stan Toler
Jeremiah 33:3

ACKNOWLEDGMENTS

Special thanks to Don Cady, Lawrence Wilson, Jerry Brecheisen, and the whole Wesleyan Publishing House team. It has been a pleasure to partner with you on this book. This project is a reflection of my Wesleyan heritage and pastoral ministry. Thanks for your rich friendship and confidence in me. Also, much appreciation to Deloris Leonard and Pat Diamond for their editorial assistance and project consultation.

PART 1

PERSONAL GROWTH

Complacency is a deadly foe of all spiritual growth.

—A. W. TOZER

I press on toward the goal to win the prize for
which God has called me heavenward in Christ Jesus.

—PHILIPPIANS 3:14

1

CHARACTERISTICS OF GREAT PASTORS

You've seen them on Christian TV. You've read their books or magazine articles. You've been to their auditorium-packed seminars. Their names are familiar. Their churches are full on the weekends and alive with activities during the week. Their church campuses resemble a small college. They are the superstars of the Church. Untold numbers of pastors have been called "good pastors," but these select few are considered "great pastors."

What makes them so great? They attended the same colleges or seminaries as other pastors. They all started out with insignificant preaching assignments. They all have mowed a church lawn or changed lightbulbs in the church basement sometime in their ministry. But the question is, does a rise in ecclesiastical stature make a great pastor? Can you be a great pastor in a smaller church? Are some pastors struggling with self-identity when, in the eyes of their parishioners, they are considered one of the greats? Of course!

A multi-thousand-member church doesn't make a great pastor. A multi-million-dollar church campus doesn't make a great pastor. A multi-degreed seminarian doesn't make a great pastor. Many pastors are great pastors in spite of all that! There is something more, something far deeper and far wider. Some have been inducted in the pastors "hall of fame" who had little of the church's recognition. Some have spent their entire ministries in bivocational pastorates and have had a greater impact for Christ than all the rest. So what's so great about great pastors?

If we look carefully, we'll see that great pastors share five essential characteristics.

They Know How to Pray

Of course there isn't a "prayer gauge." Heaven doesn't have a list of those who spend more time in prayer than others. What makes these people great in prayer? Practice. Great pastors believe in the power of prayer and practice praying on a daily basis. Practice? Is prayer a discipline—like brushing your teeth? I believe it is. You are taught something because you either don't know how to do it or because you want to improve your skill.

The disciples asked the Savior to teach them how to pray. (See Luke 11:1.) They wanted to improve their discipline of prayer. They had regularly witnessed the Son of God praying to His Heavenly Father. They saw or heard His intensity, His humility, and His dependence on His Father. They witnessed the strength He gained from those regular times of prayer, and they wanted to be like Him.

You will do many things that you thought at first were impossible because you believe God in prayer to do it through you. Great pastors understand that it is their connection to God—not their skill—that will sustain them. They are known as prayer warriors and have a prayer routine. Great pastors get out of the church "loop" and spend time alone with God, and they are more concerned about spiritual health than church health.

You may or may not have a megachurch, but you can be a giant in prayer.

They Have Personal Integrity

Unfortunately, many pastors will spend long hours on a pedestal—high enough for everyone to watch their every move. Great pastors will pass the test. They won't always do the right thing, but they will always seek one thing: Christlikeness. They will seek to be like the Master in their personal life and in their ministry. A great pastor always speaks the truth and has the courage to correct his or her mistakes. The words "I'm sorry" aren't pulled from their mouths like an impacted tooth. Great pastors take responsibility for their actions. They lead with integrity. They understand that when they're confronted with compromise, there is one right moral choice—and they are willing to make it.

Great pastors realize that they are ambassadors of the Kingdom. They make personal choices or lead others to make choices that are good for the Kingdom—good administrative choices, good ministry choices, and good relational choices. They are known for their "tough love." Their resolute demeanor has an underlying compassion that affects their every attitude or action.

They Have Great Flexibility

Great pastors understand that their way isn't necessarily the best way. They copy the best of the best—unless it compromises their character or calling. Leadership in any arena comprises two components. The first is technical expertise, or the ability to get the job done. It is important for a pastor to be proficient in the skills of his or her discipline. Great pastors are willing to step out onto the ecclesiastical edge. They are willing to do things differently if the end result is the building up of the Kingdom.

They Are Team Builders

But there is another component of their leadership. Great pastors are willing to pass the torch to a new generation. And they surround themselves with eager learners. These leaders are mentors as well as learners, help-ing those around them learn what they have mastered.

They Have a Sense of Direction

Great pastors know how to clarify their vision. The Apostle Paul had the unique ability to focus his energies on what really mattered. First and foremost, he focused on Christ. Great pastors have a well-grounded sense of identity. They seek the direction of the Holy Spirit in their lives and in their ministries.

Great pastors are willing to lead their people into unmapped terri-tory if God designs it. They know where they are going and they are willing to take others with them.

They Have a Great Commitment

They know that they could have excelled in other vocations. But great pastors understand that they have more than a job. They know they have answered the call of God. They accept the risks that come with their calling and are willing to pay a price to succeed. They have counted the cost of answering their call, and they do not look back.

Great pastors aren't great because of the size of their church. They're great because of their commitment to excellence.

Does that describe you?

2

Discovering Joy
in Ministry

Leadership involves the management of people, projects, and property. It can be done in a spirit of duty—or dread—and it can be done in a spirit of enthusiasm. Enthusiasm always trumps dread. Joy is the missing link in the lives of many leaders. For too long they have been trying to pay their "dos" with emotional credit cards that have reached their limit. To give oneself for the benefit of another out of pure joy is a rarity.

Great leaders find a way to make deposits in their emotional bank. They have a reserve account of joy. Isn't joy the true calling of every New Testament-style leader? Consider these Scripture verses:

"Until now you have not asked for anything in my name. Ask and you will receive, and your joy will be complete" (John 16:24).

"The disciples were filled with joy and with the Holy Spirit" (Acts 13:52).

"May the God of hope fill you with all joy and peace as you trust in him, so that you may overflow with hope by the power of the Holy Spirit" (Rom. 15:13).

"In all my prayers for all of you, I always pray with joy" (Phil. 1:4).

What's the secret to maintaining joy? Try these tips.

Give More Than You Get

Don't allow a "what about me?" attitude to invade your thinking. Consider yourself a giver, someone who adds value to others. Look to contribute more than you receive. It doesn't take much to add joy to someone's life. It can be done with a smile, a small gift from a recent trip, a surprise e-mail of appreciation, or a plastic trophy put on someone's desk in their absence. People need to feel that they are just as valuable to the team as the leader is. Only the leader can make them feel that way.

Jesus was a joy giver. Wherever He went and in whatever He did, people were always the better for it. It wasn't just about miracles. It was about heavenly enthusiasm even in the earthly mundane. It was about leaving a place in better shape than He found it. A word of praise or affirmation or love or forgiveness brought sunshine to hearts on their cloudy days.

Keep Your Heart Hot

When you keep a woodstove hot, not much soot builds up in the chimney. When your heart is hot, there's very little room for pride, envy, jealousy, and other joy killers. When Moses met with Jehovah God, he had to veil his face for the trip home. God's presence burned so brightly in his heart that it made his face shine. Leaders need those kinds of appointments. In fact, they are the most important dates on their PDAs or iPods. Time alone with God. Time to kindle the flame. Time to stir the coals of commitment. Time to let God's glory fill the heart. Keep the phone lines to heaven burning with your prayers. Let the fire of the Holy Spirit burn within you. Joy will follow.

Narrow Your Focus

Often joy lies buried. It's beneath that pile of papers—always there, but not visible because of the pile. The problem is you are probably the one who stacked that pile on your desk. Of course, some of the papers were handed to you. But many times, you "adopted" them. The most frustrated leaders are usually those who attempt too much. In case you haven't heard, you cannot be all things to all people. Trim your portfolio down to the essentials. Major on your strengths and delegate the tasks at which you are weakest. You'll enjoy your work a lot more.

Give Joy Away

Joy is a boomerang. When you give it away, it always comes right back. Give away all the joy you can, and your cup will soon overflow. Praise the achievements of teammates. Be quick to offer a kind word. Become a person who makes others feel good about themselves, and they will return the favor. Some of your most trusted workers, and hardest workers, are those who have feelings of inferiority. They've been chained to the words of family members, friends, or enemies. Their joy was stolen from them. They need it back. You can't give them their original joy, but you can give them a wonderful replacement. You can be the motivator that was never present in their life. You can be the source of affirmation they never had.

Surprisingly, when you give to those who lack, you gain it back. In affirming others, for example, you receive affirmation. Jesus said, "Give, and it will be given to you. A good measure, pressed down, shaken together and running over, will be poured into your lap. For with the measure you use, it will be measured to you" (Luke 6:38). Random acts of joy giving will result in ongoing joy. Try it!

When a leader does not enjoy his or her assignment, the entire organization works under a cloud. Your emotional well-being is critical to the success of your mission. Put the missing link back into your leadership. Recapture joy.

3

Reflecting the Holiness of God

Do you remember the first time you heard your own voice recorded and played back? You probably reacted like so many others: "Do I really sound like that?" Or, have you ever had a picture taken, and when it was developed you remarked, "That doesn't look like me"?

Isaiah had a similar struggle with sight and sound.

> In the year that King Uzziah died, I saw the Lord seated on a throne, high and exalted, and the train of his robe filled the temple. Above him were seraphs, each with six wings: With two wings they covered their faces, with two they covered their feet, and with two they were flying. And they were calling to one another: "Holy, holy, holy is the LORD Almighty; the whole earth is full of his glory." At the sound of their voices the doorposts and thresholds shook and the temple was filled with smoke.
>
> "Woe to me!" I cried. "I am ruined! For I am a man of unclean lips, and I live among a people of unclean lips, and my eyes have seen the King, the LORD Almighty" (Isa. 6:1–5).

Isaiah saw the holiness of God and heard the reaction of the adoring angels in its presence. Isaiah then looked at himself and said, "That doesn't look like me. I don't sound like that." C. S. Lewis wrote, in *Letters to an American Lady*, "How little people know who think that holiness is dull. When one meets the real thing . . . it is irresistible." Isaiah gave us a glimpse of the wholly genuine seated on a throne, high and exalted. Looking so out of place in God's presence, the prophet expressed an agonizing longing to reflect what God truly is—holy. But what does holiness look like?

I'm glad God solved the problem by giving us a glimpse of himself in His Word—as much as we can stand this side of eternity. "For since the creation of the world God's invisible qualities—his eternal power and divine nature—have been clearly seen, being understood from what has been made, so that men are without excuse" (Rom. 1:20).

In the Old Testament, He is seen in the awesome and unapproachable majesty of the throne, the burning bush, and the ark of the covenant. Later, in the New Testament, He is seen in the redemptive vulnerability of the animals' manger, the executioner's cross, and the borrowed grave. Holiness characterizes God. And holiness must be reflected in His people—especially in the lives of His ministers. "It is written: 'Be holy, because I am holy'" (1 Pet. 1:16).

It seems implausible at first. Reflecting God's holiness? Because of who He is, He could never be like us. But also because of who He is, He invites us to be like Him. The impossible becomes possible through the provision of His Son, Jesus Christ, and the power of His Holy Spirit. Wesley said the Holy Spirit is the "immediate cause of holiness."

How then should we reflect God's holiness?

First, God's holiness is reflected in an unconditional hatred of sin. Proverbs 6:16–19 reads, "There are six things the LORD hates, seven that are detestable to him: haughty eyes, a lying tongue, hands that shed innocent blood, a heart that devises wicked schemes, feet that are quick to rush into evil, a false witness who pours out lies and a man who stirs

up dissension among brothers." Reflecting God's holiness means rejecting sin. "No one who lives in him keeps on sinning. No one who
continues to sin has either seen him or known him" (1 John 3:6).

Second, God's holiness is reflected in an unconditional love for His
people. "How great is the love the Father has lavished on us, that we
should be called children of God!" (1 John 3:1). God's heart looks
beyond the deed to the doer. He can't accept the sin, but He can wrap
His arms of acceptance and forgiveness around the repentant sinner.
Reflecting God's holiness means that we do not exclude others. That
doesn't mean stamping approval on sin—in any form. It does mean,
however, having a heart that is inclusive rather than exclusive. In his
message titled "The Way of Holiness," Jonathan Edwards declared that
the way "is sweet and ravishingly lovely."

Third, God's holiness is reflected in unconditional sacrifice for the
welfare of others. John 3:16 has been mocked by football fans, wrestling
promoters, and stand-up comedians. But it will never be replaced as the
definitive word on God's commitment to His creation. Reflecting God's
holiness means putting aside self and selfishness for the redemption of
others. According to Paul the apostle, that is seen in the home as well as
on the highways. Ephesians 5:25 admonishes us: "Husbands, love your
wives, just as Christ loved the church and gave himself up for her."

Though we are not "little gods," as some religions teach, we can
have a little of God in us. "It is because of him that you are in Christ
Jesus, who has become for us wisdom from God—that is, our righteousness, holiness and redemption" (1 Cor. 1:30).

As John Brown, a nineteenth-century Scottish theologian, wrote,
"Holiness consists in thinking as God thinks, and willing as God wills."
What is that? Reflecting the holiness of God!

4

KEYS TO
FLAWLESS CHARACTER

The farmer pulled his truck onto the scales at the grain elevator and then stepped out of the cab. Just as the scale operator was about to take his reading, the farmer stepped quietly onto the scale, adding his weight to that of his crop. Believing no one had seen him, the farmer then emptied his truck and returned to the scale to retrieve his receipt.

Although the scale operator had noticed the farmer's sly action, he chose not to confront the dishonesty directly. Instead he handed the receipt to the farmer and said, "I thought you might like to know, you just sold yourself for eight dollars and fifty-six cents."

A leader's character is always on display. Every day, you and I are observed making dozens of choices, large and small. Our employees notice whether or not we treat others fairly. The public observes how we respond to criticism. Our families see whether our private actions match our public words.

Your character counts.

History will not judge your leadership according to what you know or even what you have accomplished. Your legacy will be determined by who you are. If you are a leader with great character, your influence will far outlast you.

Yet the character of a leader is under constant attack. Leaders are not immune to temptation. In fact, there are some ways in which we seem even more vulnerable to Satan's assaults. The pressure on leaders and their families has only increased in recent years.

You have begun your mission with the best of intentions. You can finish the same way. Here are four essential checks on a leader's character. Keep these sentinels in place, and you are sure to be a leader who is worthy of being followed.

Self-Define

Leadership expectations have exploded in the past decade. Organizations of all types expect more from their leaders, and leaders demand more from themselves. The pressure to perform is stressful at best, punishing at worst. The leader who survives those escalating pressures will be the one who has a clear-cut job description and communicates it well within the organization. You must understand who you are and what you are called to do. You need to have a clear sense of your mission as a leader. Create your own definition of success; don't allow others to assign one to you. Determine who you are as a leader, and don't try to be something you are not.

Self-Examine

Perhaps this era will be known as the Great *Distraction*. Never before has so much evil opportunity presented itself. The media has bombarded us with the message that whatever feels good is ultimately good. Of course, there is significant danger in that philosophy—especially for the Christian leader.

The traditional advice to a young leader on dealing with sexual temptation goes something like this: "Never allow yourself to be alone with a person of the opposite sex." That nostrum implies that sexual attraction is an irresistible force that might attack the unwary leader by surprise. Once alone in the presence of a person of the opposite sex, the leader might be helpless to resist temptation.

In reality, sexual integrity, like any other character issue, has more to do with what is inside than what is outside. In other words, it's the leader's heart condition, rather than the attractiveness of another person, that creates the temptation.

Better advice to the leader is to understand yourself. When you are lonely, discouraged, or vulnerable, admit it and deal with the issue appropriately. Being honest, even with yourself, about issues such as rejection, insecurity, and low self-esteem is a vital skill for survival in a highly pressurized vocation.

Self-Discipline

Most people have one or two glaring weaknesses. Very few people seem to be weak in all areas. Some of us seem genetically prone to use addictive substances such as alcohol. Others have no problem with alcohol but will lie or steal if necessary to acquire money. Wise people, and certainly wise leaders, have an understanding of their own psyche. They know what makes them tick. They know what tempts them, and they learn to keep those desires in check. They have mastered their weaknesses in order to maximize their strengths.

Self-Report

It is not new advice, but it is still worth hearing. Get an accountability partner. Find someone you can trust, and give that person permission to ask you about anything—your marriage, your finances, your personal habits, and your interactions with the opposite sex. Here are some good accountability questions: (1) Is there any unconfessed sin in your life? (2) What is your greatest spiritual struggle right now?

(3) What do you think you need to do in order to avoid sin in that area?

(4) Have you prayed since we last met?

Great achievement plus weak character equals disaster. Keep your character strong, and your influence will be just as strong.

5

STEPS TO

PASTORAL HEALTH

7:15 a.m. A phone call. The treasurer has a question and needs the information before leaving for work. You check the budget file while wiping shaving cream from your face. "I hope I didn't get you out of bed," the caller remarks—as if a telephone survey were being taken.

8:40 a.m. An unscheduled office visitor interrupts your sermon preparation. Her snapshots of the Grand Canyon are truly breathtaking. She forgets that she showed you the pictures after the midweek service—last week.

9:30–11:00 a.m. Staff meeting runs overtime dealing with conflict in the youth ministry area of the church. You know you won't have enough time to settle the turf battle, but you make one last stand.

11:30 a.m. You return phone calls until your lunch appointment arrives—glad you have those extra minutes on your cell phone contract.

12:00–1:30 p.m. Lunch with a board member who lays out his vision for the church, and it's not exactly the same as yours. In spite of the differences you pick up the tab.

2:00–3:00 p.m. Premarital counseling appointment.

3:30–4:30 p.m. Meeting with claims adjustor concerning water damage to the church basement. You're tempted to talk to him about the Flood, but you don't know if dropping Noah's name will give you an advantage.

4:30 p.m. Parishioner calls as you're leaving the office. Comments, "I wish my day ended this early." Last week her oldest child asked you what you did as a full-time job.

5:00–6:30 p.m. Family time. You eat dinner, help with homework, hear about your wife's day, and balance the checkbook.

7:00–9:00 p.m. Midweek service. You greet the people, settle a dispute between children's workers, remind board members about tomorrow's meeting, conduct a Bible study, give impromptu counsel to a harried parent, and shut off the lights.

9:20 p.m. Your last phone call. Parishioner wants to thank you for visiting his mother in the nursing home. He says, "It's wonderful that you have so much free time."

Your schedule is filled with meaningful activity, but it's hectic. In giving your life for others, you and your family are liable to be lost in the shuffle. You care for others, but who takes care of you?

Here are self-care basics that will help you shine bright without burning out.

Get Enough Rest

Many pastors don't sleep enough. Especially in a growing church, there is a very real temptation to burn the candle at both ends. We run from office hours to committee meeting to Bible study. Twelve-hour days and sixty-hour weeks are not uncommon for pastors.

Stop it!

God created us as fragile human beings. Learn to say no, take time for yourself, and get some rest.

Take Time Off

Some pastors feel guilty when they relax. Don't. Most laypersons enjoy that most wonderful of modern creations every week: the weekend. Pastors must force themselves and their churches to accept the fact that their schedule is not typical. They need permission (sometimes from themselves) to take a day off in the middle of the week or spend an afternoon with family. Schedule a consistent time off every week. Put it in your date book, and then do it.

Develop Close Friendships

Isolation is common in the ministry. Pastors are often separated from their extended family members. Their social lives are usually limited to interaction with parishioners. It may take some effort, but it's worth the work to identify a friend outside your congregation and build a relationship. Isolation is dangerous. Reach out and touch someone.

Pursue a Hobby

Tennis. Fly-fishing. Woodworking. Golf. Camping. Antiquing. Photography. Every pastor should find something other than work to occupy a portion of his or her time. It will free the mind, ease stress, and provide a sense of achievement.

Maintain a Devotional Life

Pastors pray for a living, but they must also pray to survive. It's disgustingly easy for us to become "professional" Christians. Make the effort to acquire personal spiritual disciplines that don't relate to public ministry. Keep a journal. Find a mentor. Make a retreat. You'll help yourself and your family.

Seek Help When You Need It

You don't have to go it alone, and you shouldn't try. It's difficult for the caregiver to accept care, but sometimes it's necessary. If you feel isolated, find a friend. If you're fatigued, go to the doctor. If you have a spiritual or emotional problem, see a counselor. It's true that we are all wounded healers. Don't be afraid to ask for help when you need it.

In your mission to cure souls, don't neglect your own. Your family loves you. The Kingdom needs you. Your parishioners depend on you.

Pastor, take care of yourself.

6

CREATING A DYNAMIC
DEVOTIONAL LIFE

In sports, there's something called "two-a-days," and nobody likes them! Athletes are forced to rise early and practice all morning, running sprints, drills, and exercises until they don't know if they'll find enough oxygen in the air to survive. Then, after a few hours of recuperation, they come back for a second session made even more strenuous by the afternoon heat.

Although extremely tough for the moment, each athlete knows this rigorous training will give him or her a competitive edge. Disciplined athletes will not only go through this grueling ordeal once; they'll return day after day for more! They'll be ready for each contest, and they'll succeed.

Just as the competitor cannot win without physical discipline, neither can we succeed as pastors without spiritual discipline. Like Jesus, we need a consistent practice of prayer, solitude, Scripture reading, and fasting. We need food for our souls.

I know that many of you struggle, like the athlete, to maintain discipline in your spiritual life.

Perhaps you have determined to establish a consistent prayer time or to read Scripture, not only for sermon preparation but also to nurture your heart. You may have decided to fast regularly, to meditate, to spend time alone with God. Any one of these can be the greatest commitment you can make to your ministry.

There are a number of reasons that churches do not grow—location, sacred cows, poor facilities, and so forth. But perhaps the most logical reason is identified in Jeremiah 10:21: "The shepherds are senseless and do not inquire of the Lord; so they do not prosper and all their flock is scattered." Prayerlessness! Prayer is the most important thing a pastor has to do every day.

Missionary statesman J. Hudson Taylor said, "The power of prayer has never been fully tried in any church. If we want to see the mighty wonders of divine grace and power, instead of weakness failure and disappointment, the whole church must accept God's standing challenge: 'Call unto me, and I will answer thee, and shew thee great and mighty things, which thou knowest not' (Jer. 33:3 KJV)."

Jesus taught us to pray for a reason—to tap in to the matchless grace, the magnificent promises, and the marvelous resources of Almighty God. Why? Not only are we equipped to fulfill the call, but also we are fulfilled. Jesus' prayer disciplines led Him from the Mount of Olives to the Garden of Gethsemane. It brought Him inner peace and connection to His Heavenly Father, and it reinforced His commitment to do the Father's will.

Here are six important keys to a vibrant payer life.

Pray Daily

In today's fast-paced ministry environment, it's tempting to make prayer a B item on your action list. After all, we have so much to do. But prayer is worthy of the A list. It's your source of strength. You can't succeed without it. Pray today, and make the resolve to pray every day.

Pray First

If you put your prayer time late in the day, something is sure to invade the time. Phones ring, visitors drop in, schedules get rearranged. Pray first or you might not pray at all. Set your alarm thirty minutes earlier than usual. Open your Bible before your day planner. Make prayer the first action item each day.

Pray Up

Most of our prayers have a "down here" focus. We pray for ourselves, for our needs, for the things we'd like today. Our prayers can be quite selfish when our focus is this side of heaven. Try praying "up." Focus on the Father. Praise Him. Honor Him. Glorify Him. Spend some time simply bragging on God. Come into the glory of His presence. You'll be uplifted in the process.

Pray Out

There is no question but that you should pray for yourself. When you have a need, you can and should take it to the Father. But most prayers should go "out" on behalf of others rather than "in" on ourselves. Praying for my needs is seldom as invigorating as praying for the needs of others. Take your membership roll with you to your prayer session. Call out the names—and needs—of your constituents as you pray.

Pray Big

Do you have a mustard seed's worth of faith? I'm sure you have at least that much! And that's enough to move a mountain! When you pray, ask for God to accomplish great things through you. Pray, believing that God will be as good as His Word. Remember, you're speaking to "him who is able to do immeasurably more than all we ask or imagine" (Eph. 3:20). Pray big prayers and get ready to see God do big things!

Pray Constantly

A dedicated prayer time is important; an attitude of prayer is vital. "Pray without ceasing," Paul instructed us (1 Thess. 5:17 KJV). Let prayers rise from your heart throughout the day—in thanks for daily bread, in petition for protection, in praise for the day, in instant confession of sin. Your most important drive-time activity isn't listening to the radio or tunes on an iPod. Pray as you go. Be in a constant attitude of dependence on God. Let His Holy Spirit bring the truth of the Word to your heart. Let the compassion of Christ direct your thoughts toward others.

Pray. Don't go another day without a vibrant experience of prayer. Assess your prayer life and make changes as needed. Even if your ministry is thriving, no minister ever prayed too much or experienced too much of God!

7

FACING PERSONAL ATTACKS

Pastors are easy targets for criticism and malicious attacks. You can recognize those who are getting the job done—they're the ones with arrows in their backs. Here are some tips for facing the rumors or the rummaging of parishioners or even other leaders. But more importantly, here are some tips for facing personal attacks.

Develop a Thick Skin

Remember that some harsh remarks come with the territory of leadership, and they shouldn't always be taken seriously. When things go wrong, people complain about the leader; what else can they do? If they complain about their boss, they may soon be in the unemployment line. It's easier to complain about someone when a paycheck isn't involved. Who's next in line? The pastor. He or she won't get rid of you. Your tithe is too important, or there are too many of your family members in the church. Besides, pastors have been on the receiving end of criticism since the birth of the Church.

Develop a thick skin. Understand the source. Look beyond the words. Remember that the person has his or her own problems, which may be translated into verbal darts.

Keep focused on the goal, and don't forget that your Leader, Jesus, endured the same kinds of abuse. Can the servant be above his or her Lord? Of course not! The same Savior who promised never to leave your side has walked your path. The taunts rang in His ears. The doubts even invaded the minds of His closest disciples. Discipline yourself to ignore the potshots and snide comments that are directed at *every* leader.

Develop a Short Memory

One of the best things you can do is learn to forget—not the lessons of the past, but its insults. Remember that you can forgive, because you have been forgiven. Allow your attackers a way out. Give them room to retract remarks made in the heat of an argument. Be willing to forgive and forget. Tom Elliff, past president of the Southern Baptist Convention, said that he who cannot forgive breaks the bridge over which he himself must pass. When you let others off the hook for their failures, they'll be more tolerant of yours.

You don't have to look very far to find the best example. In His hours of deepest distress, hanging on a cross that was undeserved for a people who were unworthy, the heart of the Master was broken for His tormentors. Perhaps some of the sweetest words ever spoken came from the cross: "Father, forgive them." He is living His life through you. What and whom you cannot forgive, He can.

Develop a Fan Section

Every leader needs cheerleaders, the people who can build them up when they're feeling down. These are not yes-men who shower a leader with false praise, but true friends whose counsel can be trusted. Again, you won't have to look very far. Remember the family members who will stand by you no matter what. Remember the spouse who is still cheering you on, even when he or she is on the same battlefield as you.

For every person who doubts you, there are a hundred who believe in you. Often they are overlooked. The friends you've had all your life. The people from your last ministry assignment who listened to your counsel and experienced change for the better. That prayer warrior on whose prayer list you have been since the beginning of your ministry. They're for you!

Oh, and don't forget the people in your present assignment whose lives have been changed through your ministry. The boy or girl in your Christian education program who wants to grow up to be just like you. The parents who haven't forgotten your all-night stay with them in the hospital room of their child. The teen whose life was turned around by your forgiveness and friendship. They're for you!

When it seems that the whole world is weighted against you, it's important to have a few friends who can tip the scales by giving needed affirmation. Develop a cadre of honest supporters, and rely on their candid advice.

Develop a Forward Focus

Don't dwell on the past; there's no future in it. If the goals you're pursuing are worth reaching, they must be more important than fighting ego battles, being proven right, or seeking revenge. You can't navigate when you're looking in the rearview mirror. Keep your eyes on the prize.

I once asked a prominent leader how he was able to tolerate the insults that go along with public life, and his answer was stunning. "I don't have time to be bitter," he said. "I only have time to be better." So it is with you. You are doing the most important work in the world—bringing hope and healing to the hurting. There are greater things to do than cataloging insults for your archives.

Besides, by the time you're into your next ministry assignment, your critics will be your best friends. Those who have forgotten your help will remember. Those who had the harshest words for you will be singing your praise. Time has a way of dulling even the sharpest arrows.

Give your critics room to grow. Help them grow. Show them by example that words hurt as much as sticks and stones, but you have a grace available to you to experience healing. Smile when your critics are frowning. Sing while your accusers are slinging stones. You have been given the greatest of opportunities: the opportunity to have the last word about the situation. Right may come under some vicious attacks, but it will always win.

Remember, God is for you!

8

PASTORING
THE PASTOR

An estimated fifty-one million people watched the final episode of a recent *Survivor* series, making it one of the most watched programs in television history. Sixteen people had been "stranded" on an island near Borneo. Their challenge was to eke out an existence, eating anything from bugs to bats. This summer replacement show soon became a legendary series, and each week viewers tuned in to see who would survive the insect bites and backstabbing to be the winner.

One man triumphed over all of it to become an instant millionaire. He won because he learned how to adapt, took the time to understand people, and refused to be sidetracked by the pressures of the island and the personalities of the island dwellers.

These days, ministry can seem like a game of survivor. We live in an age of scandals, moral failures, creeping criticism, and increasing threats to our value system. The rules keep changing, and so do ministry methods. What worked in the 1970s, or even the 1990s, may not be effective today. Our culture exerts more and more influence, and we're often scrambling to stay in the game!

Our mission, however, has not changed. This culture needs Christ. Our task is to reach the millions who still haven't heard the good news. Those who will be effective are those who learn to adapt, to understand people, to avoid distractions, to handle the pressures, to cope with change to survive! That's a challenge you can meet. No one can vote you off this island. You're in this ministry for the long haul—and you're not alone.

One pastor recently estimated that 80 percent of the clergy in his denomination have thought about giving up the ministry sometime in the past month. Whether that number is realistic or not, the fact is that many pastors are ready to quit. Unrealistic expectations and mounting obligations are taking their toll. But there are ways to strengthen yourself and your ministry. You need not just survive; you can actually thrive in ministry.

In a day when nobody "pastors" the pastor, you need to get good at taking care of yourself. There's no quick fix, but you can be successful over the long haul if you will get good at five things. Master these endurance skills, and you'll master the ministry.

Howard Hendricks said that if you stop learning today, you stop teaching tomorrow. Think of yourself as a lifelong learner. Make the decision that you will not be satisfied with the personal and professional skills that you now have—that you'll keep growing. Read constantly. Books, magazines, journals—read anything you can get your hands on. Feed your mind with good ideas.

Acquire computer skills. A pastor who can use common software applications such as a word processor, spreadsheet, desktop publisher, and the Internet can double his or her productivity and discover new ministry possibilities.

Pursue educational opportunities, travel, and networking with other professionals: Expand your horizons in any way you can. If you keep growing, your ministry will too.

Nobody needs another pastoral shipwreck story, so I won't share one. We all know the dangers. But few of us seem to know how to defend against them. Being honest with yourself about internal issues such as rejection, loneliness, pride, or low self-esteem is the first step to avoiding failure. Know yourself, and you won't be taken by surprise. Most people have one or two glaring weaknesses. Wise people, and certainly wise pastors, know where they are vulnerable, and they avoid temptation in those areas.

Until we see Christ face to face, stay focused on God's mission. Stay true to yourself and those you love. Brace yourself for the taunts and temptations of the Enemy. And get ready for a celestial homecoming beyond your wildest dreams!

9

POWERING UP FOR
MINISTRY

When it comes to navigation, the great patriarch, Abraham, was a lot like Christopher Columbus on his journey to a new land. He didn't know where he was going when he started out, and he didn't know where he was when he got there. "By faith Abraham, when called to go to a place he would later receive as his inheritance, obeyed and went, even though he did not know where he was going" (Heb. 11:8).

Abraham may not have known *where* he was going, but he knew *why*. God had called him. God's plan was now Abraham's purpose. And spiritual purpose was a great motivator in the life of the man who was called a "friend of God."

Though we are busier than ever, many of us live our lives rather aimlessly at times—even though our intentions are noble. At work, we desire to be the consummate professional. At home, we seek to be the ultimate spouse or parent. At church, we are the devout believer. In spite of our involvement, it often seems that there's something missing in our lives. We lack power.

A consecrated life is a life devoted to a single purpose. Like Abraham, it settles on God's plan, no matter the consequence. What may we expect from such a consecrated life? What is the result of consecrating our life to Christ, making His will our main objective? In a word, power.

That power rises from an increased focus. When you understand the big picture, it's easier to put the little things in place. A consecrated life is focused on serving God. That makes every decision—from vocational choices to moral decisions—much easier to make. Consecration brings the power of focus.

That power also produces great endurance. There is no more noble cause than Christ's—no more valid reason to persevere in spite of pain or persecution. When your life has been laid at the feet of the Master, when His cross is squared firmly across your shoulders, you will have the strength to face life even at its worst. Insults are easier to bear, sacrifices easier to make. Consecration brings the power of endurance.

That power brings certain victory. That term may be as obsolete as an Edsel at times, but victory is still the believer's greatest incentive. Paul put the promise in writing: "Thanks be to God, who always leads us in triumphal procession in Christ and through us spreads everywhere the fragrance of the knowledge of him" (2 Cor. 2:14). The consecrated person is a victorious soldier for Christ—even before the battle begins. Whether the struggle is against temptation in his or her own life or against the forces of spiritual darkness in the world, the believer with a single focus is able to endure. Consecration brings victory.

The Scriptures bear it out. The writer of Hebrews mentioned other "Hall of Faith" Christians who had consecrated themselves to God. Those who had placed their lives on the altar of devotion and let them burn; others who were hopelessly devoted to their God. What was the result in their lives? Just read on.

"And what more shall I say? I do not have time to tell about Gideon, Barak, Samson, Jephthah, David, Samuel and the prophets, who through faith conquered kingdoms, administered justice, and gained what was promised; who shut the mouths of lions, quenched the fury of the flames, and escaped the edge of the sword; whose weakness was turned to strength; and who became powerful in battle and routed foreign armies" (Heb. 11:32–34).

And there is one name missing from that list: yours. By faith, you, too, may become one of these of whom the world was not worthy. By faith, you, too, may be consumed by a passion for God that burns away every thought, every motive that is not focused on His will. By faith, you may endure any hardship, achieve any victory. By faith, you may prevail.

That's not to say that you won't be tempted to quit. In fact the devil will sing that song in your ear frequently. He wants to destroy you—and your ministry. You will have to guard your heart and your mind against his attacks. How?

Remember, God called you.

Remember what God did for you. You have been translated from the kingdom of darkness to the kingdom of light through faith in the Lord Jesus Christ.

Remember what God promised you. God redeemed you and called you by His grace. Every spiritual provision has been made available to you.

Remember what God has promised you. Your work is noted in heaven. And your work will be rewarded in heaven. You may not receive a single word of encouragement on earth, but as the expression says, you're not home yet.

The consecration of your life to the service of the Lord is only a beginning. Each day brings a new sense of belonging and victory. That's the power of a consecrated life.

10

MAKING A
GOOD IMPRESSION

P roper attire required," the sign on the restaurant door read. In other words, people who aren't properly dressed aren't welcome. If that is true in a restaurant, it is more so in the church. Your appearance will either gain you entrance into the hearts of your church or it will keep you from them.

Of course, the gospel is for everyone, of every means. You wouldn't deny someone entrance to your church if they were dressed shabbily. You are inclusive because the gospel is inclusive. On the other hand, you probably wouldn't put that shabbily dressed person on the praise team without a little wise counsel.

Ministers are ambassadors of heaven. "We are therefore Christ's ambassadors, as though God were making his appeal through us" (2 Cor. 5:20).

Would you expect to see the ambassador of a foreign country representing that country at a public gathering dressed in the clothes that he or she wore to work in the garden? Of course not! The ambassador's *apparel* is a reflection of the ambassador's *association*.

The workplace used to allow a "casual Friday." It's interesting to note that even that policy has been amended. For many corporations, casual is no longer cool. Let's face it; the emergent church is a casual church. The weekend services are no longer an "Easter parade." But Christian leaders will still exercise caution when it comes to their appearance. What appearance standards should be observed by today's ministers? Let's consider a few.

Be Neat

The shabbiest looking person in a hospital room shouldn't be the pastor of the local church! Ambassadors aren't usually seen at public gatherings wearing flip-flops, tank tops, or cutoffs. A standard of neatness is observed.

Of course neatness has as much to do with cleanliness as it does with clothing. Need we be reminded that neatness includes proper hygiene? I know of a gifted preacher who always stood nose to nose with those to whom he was speaking. The trouble was he had bad breath. Looking back, I believe that man's ministry would have had a wider influence if he had simply carried some breath mints with him— and used them more often than not.

Neatness also has to do with the appearance of your clothing. Clean. Pressed. Color coordinated. Changed regularly. Most seminaries don't offer a Clothing 101 course, but maybe they should. It doesn't matter how many letters you have after your name, if you dress like a slob you'll have a tougher time being effective in ministry. Look around. God's creation is orderly. The stars glitter. The sands are smoothed. The flowers are fragrant. The trees are beautifully coiffed. Shouldn't God's highest creation reflect that orderliness? I think so.

Dress Appropriately

I realize that most congregations don't have a dress code anymore. But there is some apparel that doesn't even belong in the supermarket, let alone the place of worship. You can be casual without being sloppy. "Anything goes" doesn't go everywhere. The Christian minister may reflect the congregation in dress, but he or she should be on the high side of the fashion equation.

Some ministry situations call for a higher standard of dress. Casual is usually out for funerals or weddings. No matter their religious background, most people expect the attending minister at such events to be "in uniform." A neat and subdued suit or dress is chosen out of respect for those honored.

Dress Simply

Whether it's right or not, some of your audience members will never hear what you say because they are focusing on what you wear. Some congregations expect their pastor to dress elegantly. Others resent it. Christian ministers should learn to discern what their congregation desires in clothing appearance. I have known some pastors who have dressed like paupers when it came time to propose a raise in salary in the church budget!

Pastors, like everyone in their congregation, should live within their means—including the money they spend on clothing.

Act Properly

Ministers can be the life of the party without being its laughing-stock. Your people want to know that religion has a light side. But that light side doesn't have to include dark humor. Tasteless stories may sound funny to some, but to most, they represent a serious problem.

Christian leaders don't have to act like everyone else to be part of the crowd. Their standard should be higher. It never hurts to add a little decorum to the gathering. In fact in some areas, decorum is *expected* of the pastor. It should never be said of a pastor that he or she "doesn't act like a pastor." Professional people reflect their profession.

Proper actions are especially important in ministering to those of the opposite sex. Flirting is out. Inappropriate comments will haunt your ministry. Close relationships to anyone of the opposite sex—other than your spouse—will destroy a lifetime of service.

And in light of the accusations or indictments regarding molestation, the pastor should never be alone with young people or children.

Unfortunately, you live in a glass house. People really are watching you. And people are comparing what you say with how you dress and act. Jesus always fit in, but He never stood out because of inappropriate words or actions.

Your influence on others is holistic. You are not partly a minister of the gospel; you are entirely a minister of the gospel. Let God guide your dress code as well as your sermon preparation. Live so that people will love the One you serve.

11

SURVIVING CHANGE

C hange changes us.

We are spiritually and emotionally vulnerable when we face changes in the routine of our lives. Vocational, housing, relationship, physical, or financial changes—all may reduce our stability to zero. The Old Testament giant, Abraham, faced unsettling uncertainty when God called him to leave his homeland and take his family to a new country.

He responded obediently: "By faith Abraham, when called to go to a place he would later receive as his inheritance, obeyed and went, even though he did not know where he was going" (Heb. 11:8). "Not knowing where he was going" is key to what he must have felt.

Change also affected his loved ones. Think about how his family must have felt. Like Abraham, they would face sad farewells, financial uncertainty, and strange situations.

Change is never easy, but it happens. When it does, our world often crumbles. Often the changes that affect us most have underlying causes. There are several.

Delayed Promises

Look at Abraham's life story. "By faith he made his home in the promised land like a stranger in a foreign country; he lived in tents, as did Isaac and Jacob, who were heirs with him of the same promise. For he was looking forward to the city with foundations, whose architect and builder is God" (Heb. 11:9–10). So, where's the city? All he saw was desert and dusty tent dwellings at the end of long travel days. Land of promise?

Delayed promises are world-crumbling situations. We thumb through the Rolodex of advice from near and far. "Just a little while . . ." "Sunday's coming." "Somewhere over the rainbow . . ."

The problem: We're used to instant coffee and microwave popcorn. Delayed promises? We're stuck in the now, like Abraham and his family, trying to eke out a life and a living.

Personal Problems

Abraham also had personal setbacks. "By faith Abraham, even though he was past age—and Sarah herself was barren—was enabled to become a father because he considered him faithful who had made the promise. And so from this one man, and he as good as dead, came descendants as numerous as the stars in the sky and as countless as the sand on the seashore" (Heb. 11:11–12).

Wouldn't it be awful to face life when you've already been declared "as good as dead"? Age and infirmity had been in a holding pattern over Abraham's life. God had made the promise: Abraham's descendants would be as numerous as the stars. But Abraham couldn't see the stars. His family would become as numerous as the sands, but all he saw was dust.

If you haven't been there, you probably will be eventually. Personal difficulties make life difficult! What are some of the symptoms? Grudges poison us. Jealousy gnaws at us. Loneliness isolates us. Inadequacies paralyze us. Finances bind us. Sorrows plague us.

Sudden Trials

Everyone in ministry has a "that day!" Abraham's life would have been so much different if it weren't for *that day*. The Scriptures say God tested Abraham (Gen. 22:1). A sudden trial arrived. God was applying a litmus test to Abraham. He wanted His protégé to see that faith works when we face *that day*.

God told Abraham to sacrifice his son. Leaving his servants behind, Abraham took the materials for the altar, along with his only son, and began the longest journey of his life. The trip from Ur was a piece of cake compared to these few steps.

"Father, where's the sacrifice?" Abraham's heart was pounding. He was committed to obey God's command. Abraham replied, "God will provide." But deep in his heart the doubts must have swirled.

That day—that sudden testing time in the life of the patriarch would be unlike any other day. Abraham passed the test. He trusted God. Then God instructed Abraham not to lay a hand on Isaac, and He provided a ram for Abraham to sacrifice.

Perhaps you've had days like that. Life was pretty uneventful, and then suddenly everything changed. A sound of metal crushing metal. A telephone call. A knock on the door. An ambulance siren. You suddenly faced a horrendous situation. Something was expected of you. Not one of us is exempt.

Underlying Feelings

Wounded healers often hide their pain. It lies festering under the surface.

Sometimes We Feel Helpless. Life is suddenly out of control; a sense of vulnerability sets in. Until now, we've been able to fix most everything else; but we can't fix this.

Sometimes We Feel Abandoned. It seems that those around us can't see our pain. "Why me, Lord?" we inquire. But often, heaven is silent.

Sometimes We Feel Worthless. Our pride and dignity are temporarily gone. Our once-secure finances are tenuous. Our once-strong bodies are frail. Our once-happy homes are in shambles. Our once-respectful children have rebelled.

Sometimes We Feel Ashamed. Perhaps we've been players, not just bystanders. We made wrong choices. We crossed the line. What now?

1. Confess. Doubting God is just as bad as disobeying Him. Admit your need. Some confessions will have to be made public; others will be made on your knees, alone with God.

2. Claim forgiveness. If your situation isn't covered by grace, then it is the only one that isn't. Of course it is covered. The Savior died for your forgiveness and healing.

3. Climb out of your rut. Take a first step in the right direction—the step of faith. Decide not to remain in the ruins. Claim the joy of the Lord as your strength.

4. Commit to ministry. Often when you need the most help, you will receive it by helping others. Your situation wasn't accidental. God knew about it before the world was formed. Use its lessons to teach others.

5. Conquer doubt. Fill your heart and mind with God's Word. Get some rest. Take a prayer walk. Listen to inspirational music. Read a book for the enjoyment and enlightenment rather than for research.

You can survive your situation. Others have. You're not alone, even when you are lonely. Your Captain, Jesus, has promised to walk with you every inch of your battlefield. And that is the victory!

12

THRIVING AMID ADVERSITY

I f it hasn't happened already, it will. There will be times in your ministry when your world seems to be coming apart. And as it was with Humpty Dumpty, it will also seem like no one around you is able to put it back together again. You may be scanning the skies to see whether the buzzards are circling overhead.

You won't be alone. As you look across any audience, there will be those who are going through world-coming-apart situations—just like you. Wondering how they can keep it together. Wondering how they can cope with the dangers of the new day.

No, Christian workers aren't immune to life's toughest questions. They may be in a tough situation, with the clouds of uncertainty on the horizon. But they're in a no-parking zone! Armed with the Word of God and the confidence of His hope they can press on.

Ministers not only have the opportunity to preach hope, they also have an opportunity to practice it. John, the disciple of Christ, looked out the window of time and caught a glimpse of eternity when he wrote, "Dear friends, now we are children of God, and what we will be has not yet been made known. But we know that when he appears, we shall be like him, for we shall see him as he is. Everyone who has this hope in him purifies himself, just as he is pure" (1 John 3:2–3). But in the meantime, you and I are called to take some steps to solidify our faith as well as our ministry.

Rest in God's Acceptance

Everywhere you look there is hopelessness, moral decay, selfishness, violence, world conflicts, you name it! But there's sunshine behind those clouds. The Lord Jesus Christ has not only seen your condition, He has also spoken these words to your heart: "You are set free." Remember, whose you are is greater than what you are going through. Isaiah spoke God's Word: "But now, this is what the LORD says—he who created you, O Jacob, he who formed you, O Israel: 'Fear not, for I have redeemed you; I have summoned you by name; you are mine'" (Isa. 43:1).

In *Mere Christianity*, C. S. Lewis defined hope as a "continual looking forward to the eternal world." One day, maybe soon, the kingdom of heaven will come to earth, and the King of Kings will reign forever and ever.

You may not be certain how or when all of that will take place. But of one thing you may be certain: You belong to the One who will have the final word. You can rest continually in the final outcome of your faith. Hold on tightly to the hope that Christ brought to your heart— every waking moment of your day.

Rest in God's Availability

The buzzards may be circling, but God's not finished with you yet. Heaven is on highest alert! Isaiah served as God's messenger: "When you pass through the waters, I will be with you" (Isa. 43:2).

Crisis only enhances lines of communication. Three church board members sat and watched a telephone repairman working in front of the church. Within earshot of the repairman, they began to discuss the best positions for prayer.

"Kneeling is definitely best," claimed one.

"Not for me," another contended. "I get the best results standing with my hands outstretched to heaven."

"You're both wrong," the third insisted. "The most effective prayer position is lying face down on the floor."

The repairman could contain himself no longer. He cupped his hands and shouted in their direction, "The best praying I ever did was hanging upside down from a telephone pole!"

The world may be upside down right now—and in your spirit, you may be hanging upside down with it. It's not a time for hand wringing, however. It's time to pray in faith. It's time to take former president of Wheaton College Victor Edman's advice: "Never doubt in the dark what God told you in the light." It's time to pack away those doubts; to put on the royal robe of righteousness. It's been freshly cleaned by the blood of the Lamb, pressed in trying times by the power of the Spirit, and paraded down the runways of time with great and mighty success.

Rest in God's Assurances

God's promises are greater than your predicament. He promised, "When you pass through the rivers, they will not sweep over you. When you walk through the fire, you will not be burned; the flames will not set you ablaze" (Isa. 43:2). The Kingdom is here now. And the Kingdom is coming as well. There may be a few buzzards circling overhead, but God hasn't failed you before, and He surely won't fail you now! There are 7,487 promises in God's Word with your name on them. God's not finished with you yet! Jesus Christ has already won your war. You don't have to look far for a hope that rises above the horrors of time. It's already yours—nonperishable, always fresh, unfading, "kept in heaven for you" (1 Pet. 1:4).

In a world of uncertainty, I urge you to take as much assurance as you will be asked to give. As you minister peace, rest in the peace that

Christ has given you. As you bind up the brokenhearted, feel His inner healing in your own soul. As you sense the loneliness of your calling, remember the constancy of His presence.

Dr. Billy Graham once said, "Our confidence in the future is based firmly on the fact of what God has done for us in Christ. No matter what our situation may be, we need never despair, because Christ is alive." Amen!

13

Improving Your Integrity

A television sitcom promo included an interesting statement by the main character: "I learned about integrity from my father. He had five wives but never missed an alimony payment."

If worldly integrity is learned by the example of careless character, we are called to a higher standard. The personal integrity of a Christian leader speaks louder than a sharp résumé, a handful of brochures, or a stack of business cards. Integrity is something that can't be handed to you as you walk across the graduation platform. Integrity comes from within. It's the result of a focused faith, godly choices, right associations, and a tenacious commitment to truth.

When integrity is present in the life of a leader, it is a beautiful thing. When integrity is missing, life gets messy! Personal integrity may be one of the least-recognized qualities for new-millennium leadership, yet it will leave the greatest legacy.

Later on, when historians think about many present-day leaders, they will struggle to remember how many people they had on their staffs and will forget how many letters followed their names. What history will remember is how leaders conducted themselves. Leaders will be known in the future primarily by their level of integrity.

In a publication called *The Cross and the Flag,* the power of integrity's legacy was chronicled in the lives of two men. One was Max Jukes, who lived as an unbeliever. Jukes had 1,029 known descendants, of whom 300 died prematurely. Of those who survived, 100 were sent to prison for an average of 13 years each; 190 were prostitutes; and 100 were alcoholics. Over the years, the Jukes family cost the state 1.2 million dollars and made no contribution to society.

The second man, Jonathan Edwards, lived in New England at about the same time as Max Jukes. He believed in God and became a prominent Christian minister. Edwards had 729 known descendants. Three hundred became preachers; 65 were college professors; 13 were college or university presidents; 60 became authors; 3 were elected to congress; and 1 became a vice president of the United States.

Integrity cannot be faked; the future will bring it to light. The most urgent question for any leader is not "What is my vision?" or "What are my skills?" The most vital issue for any leader to settle is this one: "What is my level of integrity?"

Unfortunately, integrity isn't available on eBay. Neither can you borrow it from another. It comes by diligent effort. Here are some integrity-building action points.

Determine to Never Do Anything Privately That Wouldn't Pass Public Scrutiny

Personal integrity comes from the decisions you make when no one is watching. It's decided during a TV program or a movie. It calls for the question when the computer mouse is in your hand. You make your choice by deciding what you will read when the office lights have been turned out and you're home alone.

Integrity is born in the heat of the struggle. It affects life-changing choices on the fly. Often character kicks in when you're in a counseling session or a board meeting or in a vulnerable setting. Your resistance to wrong attitudes and actions births integrity.

Determine to Never Do Anything the Scriptures Frown Upon

You don't have to look far for the way to personal integrity. It's as near as the Bible. God has filled the Book with carefully marked paths. And then He promised light for the path from the very same source.

Study the lives of biblical leaders. See what they refused. See what they gripped tightly. Copy their best. Allow the Holy Spirit to make course corrections based on biblical truth. If you will be a diligent student of integrity, you will pass the course.

Determine to Never Do Anything That Will Bring Shame to the Kingdom

You are a child of God. You are a citizen of the Kingdom. You have a reputation to uphold. The world is judging your spiritual family by your human behavior. That is a pressure point, but it's true. You carry the banner. You are a foot soldier for the Captain in the greatest battle of all.

Of course, your strength doesn't come from your resolutions. It comes from God's power that is allowed to flow freely through your life. He won't send you onto the playing field without a game plan or without the proper equipment. You belong to Him. Your safety is signed in His blood. Ask and you will receive.

Determine to Never Do Anything That Will Rob You of Your Self-Worth

Your worth has already been determined. God made you. And God's creation is perfectly assembled. You, however, will make choices that will cloud the reflection in the mirror. You will decide to purposefully unlock the door to your heart so that the "thief" will be able to steal.

You are the watchman. You will need to take action at the first sight or sound of enemy attack. Never settle for being less than who you are—and whose you are. Self-worth is the foundation upon which personal integrity stands. Keep the foundation from crumbling.

Determine to Never Do Anything That Will Make You Vulnerable to Satan

As a pastor, you're on the front lines of a great spiritual battle. Satan, the enemy, is constantly plotting your destruction, placing landmines of temptation in your way. But you don't have to be a casualty. You are old enough and wise enough to watch your step. Stay alert and you will stay alive. Watch for roaring lions clothed in cuteness or cleverness. Your personal integrity will be your legacy to those who follow you.

God forgives and forgets, but humans keep scrapbooks. Don't give them any material. Work as though being effective in ministry is entirely up to you, and live as though it depends completely upon God.

14

HOW TO GET TIME OFF

Pastor, when was the last time you had a weekend off? If you're like most, you get two full days off only once or twice a year—when you take a vacation. And how about that vacation? How do you usually spend it? Visiting in-laws? Staying with friends?

Getting time off is a problem for many clergy. We live close to the office, work weekends, and seem to have few options for travel. As a result, we're inclined to work too much. Ultimately, our health, our families, and our ministries suffer.

Resolve to get the rest and relaxation you need. Make a date with one of your best friends in ministry—your calendar. Take control of your time, and take the rest you deserve. Our task is too great to risk failure by fatigue. Relax, recuperate, and then return to work with new energy. The Lord deserves your very best!

Taking time off is not a given in the ministry. Our churches have high expectations for us, and we have high expectations for ourselves. We're driven to achieve something for the Kingdom, and we work hard at it.

And the work never stops. Phone calls come at all hours. Emergencies happen on weekends. The pastor is always on call. That means we have to be creative in taking time away from ministry. Between church schedules, family priorities, and budget constraints, finding meaningful time for relaxation can be a challenge. Here are some creative ways to get down time before you go down and out.

Work Hard

Does "work hard" sound contradictory to the advice I gave in the introduction? It's not. To take time off consistently, you'll have to discipline yourself to work diligently. Don't waste time in the office! Get to work. Avoid letting small tasks pile up so that they seem overwhelming. And keep consistent office hours. When people know that you are generally available, they're tolerant of occasional absences. But the pastor who keeps an erratic schedule may be seen as lazy. Be there when you're needed, and you can be anywhere when you're not.

Write Days Off into Your Schedule

The highest written authority for many parishioners is not the Bible but the day planner. Even those who've never heard of the fourth commandment will understand when you can't make a meeting because of a schedule conflict. They don't need to know that the "conflict" is an appointment to take your son fishing. Program days off into your BlackBerry, and then take them.

Master the Half-Day

If you must burn the candle at both ends, leave room in the middle. When you have a full evening, don't be afraid to take off the morning or afternoon. Give yourself a break, especially when evening meetings are stacked two or three days deep. Afternoons, when kids are in school, are the perfect time to pursue hobbies, read, or just relax by yourself.

Take Monday Holidays

When the kids are out of school, you should be too. Pastors already work at least half of every weekend. When Columbus Day, Presidents' Day, and other school holidays roll around, spend them with your family.

Find Time to Retreat

Look for a place you can go to be alone or with your family. Some parishioner may generously offer the use of a vacation home or condo. If an offer comes, accept gladly. But even if you don't have an exotic retreat, you can still find a quiet park, a nearby campground, or a secluded bed and breakfast. Locate a place where you and your family can enjoy complete privacy occasionally. You need it, and so do they.

Learn to Let Things Go

The work of ministry is never truly finished. In order to enjoy some down time, you'll have to live with the fact that some items remain on your to-do list. Give yourself permission to leave some tasks undone, at least overnight. Just for one day, ignore the flashing light on your answering machine and turn off your cell phone. It'll do you a world of good.

It takes discipline to relax. Few parishioners will ask whether you have enjoyed a weekend with your family recently, and most churches will not force you to take your allotted vacation time. It will be up to you to get the rest you deserve. Take it. You need it, and you'll be a better pastor for it

PART 2

FAMILY LIFE

Compassion costs. It is easy enough to argue, criticize and condemn, but redemption is costly, and comfort draws from the deep. Brains can argue, but it takes heart to comfort.

—SAMUEL CHADWICK

If anyone does not know how to manage his own family, how can he take care of God's church?

—1 TIMOTHY 3:5

15

MAKING YOUR
HOUSE A HOME

Eighteen years.

In less than two decades you'll go from being an expectant parent to being an empty nester. In less time than it takes to pay off a mortgage, your kids will graduate from a diaper to a diploma. You'll spend twenty, thirty, or forty years in pastoral ministry but only about eighteen years raising children in your home.

You must do this right.

Caring for your family is your highest priority after serving Christ.

Long before you worry about your Sunday sermon or your average attendance, spend the time it takes to be a loving spouse and a dedicated parent. Your children need you far more than your church does.

Your kids—and their kids—are going to love the Lord and His Church because of you. Not because of the sermons you preach or the board meetings you chair, but because of your first-class example as a person of faith and a parent of character.

They'll be either the best or the worst. Preachers' kids (PKs) are typically at one end of the spectrum. Either they love the Church and the ministry (a high percentage of PKs follow their parents into ministry) or they rebel against it (an alarming number fall away from faith).

What makes the difference?

While each child is responsible for his or her own choices, we know that the home life of the pastor has a tremendous influence on the faith of the pastor's child. When the parsonage is a refuge, children thrive. When the stress of church life invades the manse, children suffer.

Here are some things you can do to make your home a haven for your kids.

Be Available

Your child's most important memories won't be the high attendance days or the goals reached during a stewardship campaign. They'll remember most the times you spent with them. The main thing your children need is you. Ministry schedules are as demanding as the pastor allows them to be. A dedicated pastor may work fifty-five, sixty, or even seventy hours per week. Set a reasonable schedule. Take a day off religiously. (I'm still struggling with this one.) Guard your free evenings jealously. Let your children know that their time with you is a high priority.

Leave Church Problems at Church

Every pastor deals with conflict, stress, and difficult issues at church. One of the greatest challenges for a pastor is to go "off the clock," letting difficult issues wait until another day. Learn to leave church problems at church. Let your dinnertime conversations be about homework, Little League, or piano lessons. Don't allow the stress of the job to invade your children's lives.

Screen Your Calls

A pastor is always on call and needs to be. You need to respond to emergency situations at any time of the day. But not every phone call to the parsonage is a true emergency. Get call notes and caller ID. Don't interrupt a family video to take a call about the nursery schedule. Let the voice mail lady listen to your chronic complainers; you can call them back in the morning—maybe.

Entertain

As a pastor, you come into contact with some of the most interesting people in the world. You meet community leaders, pastors, denominational leaders, missionaries, and entertainers. Selectively invite these fascinating folk to your home for dinner or other social events. You will enrich your children's lives as you expose them to leaders from your community—and around the world!

Take Pictures

Children love to see pictures of themselves. It lets them know that they are valued. These days, you have lots of options, and you don't need to be a great photographer. Get a point-and-shoot camera, a digital camera, or camcorder. Record the good times.

Get Away

Vacations are a problem for many pastors. They don't have the income to travel to exotic places, but it's hard for a pastor to be truly off duty without leaving town. Be creative and work your networks. Find one- or two-day getaways. Get out of town once in a while. Your kids will love it, and it won't hurt your own mental health either.

Love Your Work

The largest factor in the contentment of your kids is your own attitude toward your life and ministry. When you feel frustrated or burned out, do something about it. Seek counsel, pray, evaluate your calling and your ministry situation. Keep your love for the ministry fresh, and your kids will love it too.

Growing up in a minister's home can be an incredible privilege for your children. The pastor's home can be one of the happiest places on earth. Love your kids, love your Lord, and love your work. Your house will be a bit of heaven on earth!

16

HOW TO GET ALONG WITH
ANYBODY

We live in a world where people are divided by many things—color, religion, economics, politics. Sadly, Christians are sometimes divided among themselves. When that division reaches into the home, the great task of a spouse or parent is to bring unity of purpose. In order to do that, it is sometimes necessary to mend fences, repair broken relationships, and make peace.

A benchmark is something that serves as a standard by which others are judged. Barnabas was an apostle who set the benchmark for dealing with people in a positive way. Simply put, Barnabas was an encourager. In fact, that's the nickname his fellow apostles gave him: "Son of Encouragement." He had a special gift for influencing people by overlooking their worst and bringing out their best.

Two things happened as a result. First, the early church grew because of his ministry. Second, his name is remembered and lifted up as an example for others. Learn Barnabas's secret for encouragement, and similar things will likely happen in your home. Here is the Barnabas benchmark in action. Follow these guidelines, and you'll be able to get along with just about anybody.

The Standard for Generosity

Barnabas put the necessities of others above personal niceties. On one occasion, he sold a field he owned and donated the proceeds to the apostles. (See Acts 4:36–37.) Barnabas perceived that the real needs of the New Testament Christians were more important than his real estate holdings.

Leadership in the home involves sacrifice. Often, personal plans and perks have to be put on hold to meet the immediate needs of family members. Although the Master owned the entire world, He gave it up to become our Savior. Barnabas followed that example of generosity.

The Standard for Forgiveness

When Paul (then called Saul) became a Christian, a lot of people distrusted him. After all, he had been a persecutor of the Church. But Barnabas accepted him. (See Acts 9:26–28.) Barnabas had known mercy and grace at the hand of the Galilean, and he extended that grace to others. Those who most influence their family are grace filled. They forgive others because they know that they, too, have been forgiven. They purposefully have short memories when it comes to human failures.

The Standard for Encouragement

Barnabas lived up to his nickname. He was a constant encourager of other believers. (See Acts 11:22–23.) Some leaders see the success of others as a threat. Barnabas never did. He rejoiced whenever others did well.

Look for opportunities to encourage your family. Others won't. You will have to set the standard that people will follow. Encourage your family, and they'll encourage those around them. The ripple effect will make real waves in your home, your church, your community, and beyond!

The Standard for Restoration

It was the "uncivil" war of the New Testament. When Paul and Barnabas were ready to begin their second missionary trip, they fell into a sharp dispute about a young man named John (also called Mark). Since John had deserted them once before, Paul vetoed the idea of taking John on the second trip. Barnabas, always the encourager, wanted to give the fellow one more chance. Paul and Barnabas disagreed so strongly over the matter that they agreed to part company. (See Acts 15:36–41.) Barnabas stuck with John, and the young man proved his mettle when given a second chance.

Be willing to forgive the past and give a family member another chance to succeed. Why? Because at one time or another, you have failed to meet the goals or expectations of others. You are in leadership because someone gave you another chance. You are leading by example because you are following the example of others.

Does your ministry in the home meet the Barnabas benchmark? Be generous, forgiving, encouraging, and willing to restore others, and you'll set a standard that will endure beyond that ministry.

17

MARKS OF A
HEALTHY FAMILY

The family God has put on your team was chosen beyond time. But its members didn't necessarily choose to be on your pastoral team. Slowly, or suddenly, they were put into a position where their every move is open to scrutiny by your congregation. Theirs is a staggering assignment: Be your very best while trying to be normal, and act as examples while searching for your own.

Pastor, if you've taken care of everyone in the church and neglected your family, you'll need to rearrange your priorities. Their care and keeping are at the top of your to-do list. Family priorities must come before ministry priorities. What are your family priorities? Providing godly example, teaching, encouraging, and correcting in an atmosphere of Christian love, acceptance, and moral behavior. You will also provide other things.

Financial Security

Providing financially doesn't mean handing out signed checks or credit cards without limits. You have a responsibility for helping to set the financial agenda—or at least serving as co-chairperson of the home's "finance committee!"

Learn to spot dangerous trends and make course corrections. For example, if the cashier has to use a magnifying glass to read the worn-down numbers on the credit card, then it's time to adjust the financial flow—focusing more on debit than credit. If the family's piggy bank is asthmatic from the dust that has settled on it, it's time to pay more attention to savings than cravings. If more than one family member is working more than one job just to make boat payments, it's time to board up the third door of the three-car garage—rejecting the notion that better equals more.

Stability

Your positive attitude is an anchor for the thousand storms your family will face in a post 9/11 world. There's a classic story of a little boy who was sitting in the coach section of an airplane. Soon, a storm began to shake the plane like a puppy with a knotted sock. One of the nervous passengers looked at the boy and remarked, "Son, aren't you just a little bit nervous?"

"Nope!" the boy replied confidently.

"Why not?" the passenger inquired.

"My dad's flying this thing. And this is his regular route."

Your family needs to know about your trust in God—about the faith that holds you when the storms come. They'll be in some of those storms. They will know what it is about you that gives you calm.

Affirmation

Affirming a child's gifts and graces can set the tone for your child's entire life. Verbally or nonverbally saying "I believe in you" will cause a child to believe in himself or herself. And we know by personal experience that our beliefs carry over into every area of our lives.

Affection

Many a spouse or child's inner wars have been won with a hug or a kiss. The three little words that turn houses into homes aren't "Where's the remote?" The three little words that are most important? I love you. Those hugs of affirmation at church need to be as prevalent at home.

Instruction

You probably won't teach your kids with PowerPoint presentations or writings on a chalkboard. You'll teach by your example, as well as with words. In one sense you are the family pastor. And providing life lessons based on biblical truth is in your pastoral job description.

Protection

It used to be that all the big bad wolves were only in fairy tales. Now they have an e-mail address and stroll through the ethereal avenues of the Internet with their trench-coat morals. You must be on a heightened state of alert. There really are monsters out there!

Whether you're living in a "kinder, gentler" neighborhood or a "forty-five-caliber" one, the responsibility is the same: You're on security patrol.

Protect your family from harmful attitudes. Your culture is trying to convince your family that anything goes. You have the opportunity to put some protective "wrongs" and "rights" into their minds. You'll probably need to get a head start. By the time Junior or Judy has reached the freshman dorm, it'll be too late. "Toddlerville" is a good place to put up some speed limit signs.

Protect your family from harmful addictions. Set an example in your own life. Refuse to be a part of addictive lifestyles. Preaching against excess is tougher when your comfort food becomes your constant food. Your choices in eating—or watching TV or surfing the Net or anything else—will directly affect your family.

Protect your family from harmful friendships. You know the drill: Say no to their friends and soon they'll be family. You'll need a double dose of wisdom. You'll need to know how to look beyond the pierced eyebrow of your son's date into her visionary gaze. You'll need to see beyond the lounge lizard look of your daughter's boyfriend into his soul. Sometimes you will preach a kindly message, and at other times you will pray and fast. Both have their place, with prayer being the priority.

James 1:5 says, "If any of you lacks wisdom, he should ask God, who gives generously to all without finding fault, and it will be given to him." That's right! God has promised you the right words: wisdom to say enough without saying too much; wisdom to love without giving license; wisdom to let go without going too far; wisdom to show your children how to pick their friends by the way you choose your own.

It's tough being a twenty-first-century parent or spouse. The demands are high.

Set the right priorities. Trust God. Hyperlink to His Word. Make Him the first speed-dial number in your spiritual cell phone—and call Him often. And before you know it, you'll be genuinely smiling in those graduation or wedding anniversary pictures.

18

Financial Habits for Life

They called him Penny Man, a substitute high school teacher who had an odd habit. Whenever he saw a penny lying on the floor, he would stop and pick it up. Colleagues smiled and students laughed aloud at this practice. Some even took to rolling pennies across the floor as the middle-aged teacher walked by. He faithfully stopped to retrieve every one of them.

Eccentric? Perhaps. Yet he collected several dollars a week. That teacher had learned a lesson that his teenage students seemed unable to understand: Money matters.

Money matters in your life, too. The way you handle even small amounts of it reveals something about your character. Your ability to manage your personal finances gives a clue to how you will handle business funds. These days, more than ever, leaders must have integrity in the area of finances.

Leaders are called to model the best of Christian virtues—which includes being trustworthy economically as well as morally and professionally. You probably know of someone who had the knowledge and the skills for leading people toward their mission and purpose but failed financially.

There are times when a Christian leader's integrity is compromised in the checkout lane of the corner store. A charge card under the control of the "natural" man is as dangerous as a gorilla with an acute case of indigestion! If there's one thing a leader needs to manage well, it's money.

The Apostle Peter wrote to New Testament leaders, "Be shepherds of God's flock that is under your care, serving as overseers—not because you must, but because you are willing, as God wants you to be; not greedy for money, but eager to serve" (1 Pet. 5:2). In other words, don't let your ministry be controlled by your money!

That warning is just as important in your home as it is in your church or organization. Managing finances is a life skill that every family member will need to sharpen. You are their teacher. When you practice good money management, you will encourage it in others.

Here are four habits that will keep your family on good financial footing.

Guard Your Credit Rating

Thanks to the Internet, it's easier than ever to find out what your credit score is. It's important that you know it—others do. When you apply for an auto loan, a credit card, a mortgage, or even for installment payments at the orthodontist, your credit history will be placed on display.

A good credit rating will not only save you money by placing you in line for lower interest rates and other preferred services, it will raise the opinion of those in the financial community. The bad news is that any credit problems you've had can affect your professional and personal life for several years.

Make payments on time. Never exceed the limit on your credit card. Settle disputes with creditors promptly. Your financial standing is just as valuable as your professional reputation. Guard it well.

Develop a Savings Plan

John Wesley's advice to earn all you can, save all you can, and give all you can is still at the top of the financial tips lists. It's easy to spend all the money you earn—and then some. Saving money requires careful planning and discipline. A savings or investment account balance will grow over time, but you must feed and water it with regular contributions.

If you don't plan to face a financial crisis, you plan to have one. Your car will break down. The roof on your home will need to be replaced. Someone in your family may need medical care. If you have not set aside money to deal with these eventualities, they will become emergencies.

Start small, but do start. Begin saving now, and your money will be there when it's needed most.

Resist the Irresistible

Nearly every store has impulse items placed at the checkout counter. Magazines, candy bars, soft drinks—vendors know that if you see these items you'll think, *I have to have that.*

But you don't.

Learn the difference between "need" and "want." It will save you thousands of dollars. Just because your neighbor or your colleague has the latest electronic gadget or the latest fashion fad, it doesn't mean you need it. Your neighbor or colleague may be struggling from the effects of impulse buying—and you won't even know it. Fall into their pattern, however, and you'll discover the consequences faster than you might expect.

Plan for Tomorrow Today

It'll be here before you know it, that friendly letter from the Social Security Administration reminding you that you have nearly reached retirement age. What will you do then? If you've carefully planned for retirement, you will face that day calmly. But if your impending retirement comes as a surprise, you'll likely be anxious and worried about the future.

Plan for your future now. Develop a long-term investment strategy that will pay off in the years to come. Consult a financial advisor if need be. Don't allow your golden years to become days of financial stress.

As a family leader, you will be evaluated on your performance in many areas: professional skills, personal integrity, vision clarity—and financial integrity. Develop these habits of a lifetime, and your family's financial reputation will shine as brightly as your ministry passion.

19

BRINGING OUT THE BEST IN YOUR FAMILY

Sometimes it's tempting to settle for second best. I'm reminded of the single woman who met a handsome fellow at the checkout counter and struck up a conversation. "Where do you work?" she inquired.

"Right now I'm unemployed," the man said. "I just finished a thirty-year prison sentence for armed robbery."

The lonely lady's face brightened like a neon "open" sign. "So you're single!?"

There is one place where second best just won't cut it: your family. No matter how many church growth awards you receive, if you neglect the home front you've suffered a career setback. Often family members take second chair to the plans and programs of the pastor. That must never happen. Your family must never be sacrificed on the altar of ego or acclaim. Apart from the time you spend with God, the time and energy you spend with them is your best investment. Your family deserves your best: your best effort, your best time, and your best care.

I recently overheard two mothers talking in the foyer of our church between Sunday school and the morning worship service. One mother looked a bit disheveled as she unloaded on her friend. "I just can't get my kids to do anything around the house, so I end up having to do it all—the cleaning, the dishes, the laundry, the yard work. I don't know how much longer I'm going to hold up. I'm exhausted!"

Obviously those children needed an emergency meeting of the administrative council of the home. They were showing their worst. Someone should have made it their job to look for the best in them and bring it to the surface.

Here's what you can do to bring out the best in those who live under your roof (or under the roof supplied in your salary agreement).

Love Them

Your family wants to know that you love them more than you love your parishioners. Building this assurance in them will take more than a big-ticket item from a discount store on birthdays or anniversaries. It requires a daily effort to put them first. Let family members know they are valued, they are needed, and their efforts are appreciated. The familiar saying is really true: People don't care how much you know until they know how much you care. When you love and affirm your family, they will usually do their best—because they know that they matter.

Include Them

Invite your family members to be a part of the pastoral team. Without making a big deal of it, include your family in the ministries of your church. For example, your spouse can have a major role in the friendship ministries of the church. Your children can mentor other children. Your teens can mentor other teens or be active in the children's ministry.

You're on the family coaching team. You know what skills your family members possess that will add effectiveness—without leaving out other well-qualified parishioners. Of course, this area is filled with flashing caution lights. Your task is to move on to your next church, knowing that you have built the core leadership of your past appointment. Laypersons in your church should have first dibs on church jobs, but don't overlook the skills of family members in filling the gaps.

Your spouse will be part of the counseling team whether he or she likes it or not. The concept "My mate was called to be the pastor, but I wasn't!" is ridiculous. Such conflict in roles is a spiritual problem that calls for spiritual help. Ministry couples are essentially copastors; though they usually aren't recognized as such—and certainly don't receive equal compensation.

The spouse offers one of the most important ministry assets: a listening ear (and, ideally, sealed lips). Confidential counseling between pastors and their spouses is not only key to effective ministry but also key to effective marriage relationships.

The church appointment is a co-appointment. God's leadership is usually heard in both sets of ears! Spouses whose wives or husbands don't feel the same tug of a pastoral opportunity should take a second look. God usually speaks to both hearts who are seeking His will in a ministry decision.

Teach Them

Pastor, you are a mentor to your family. Your task is to aid them in their understanding of who they are and what they can do for heaven's sake. Often family members become discouraged because they don't know what is expected of them.

Let your family members in on the mission statement. Outline the overall goals you are striving to reach. Cast a vision in the home as well as in the church. Define your objectives at their level of understanding.

A single well-directed pass can win a football championship. One well-coached family can revolutionize a ministry effort—even an entire church!

Stand by Them

You encourage your family by your words and actions. You sing their praises to the folks in the bleachers. In your eyes—and in your heart—your family team is the best. Certainly they will drop the ball once in a while. Certainly their skills will be called into question (just like yours). But that doesn't mean you let the critics call the shots. Encourage your family in public and stick up for them in private. Your loyalty will be contagious.

Christian families are on the chopping block these days. Don't let your family be one of the casualties. If individual family members fall apart at the seams—and they sometimes will—don't let it be because of your failure to build a good foundation and apply patches.

You are leading a crowd toward the eternal Kingdom. Make sure you've given your best to put your family at the front of the march.

20

HOW TO MAKE OTHERS
FEEL IMPORTANT

Cosmetics mogul Mary Kay Ash once said, "Everyone has an invisible sign hanging around his neck saying 'Make Me Feel Important!' Never forget this message when working with people." Your family members are wearing the same sign.

Two of Jesus' disciples, James and John, displayed a classic case of sibling rivalry when they tried to get Jesus to promote them ahead of their fellow apostles. Instead of a harsh lecture, however, Jesus gave them all a lesson in humble leadership. (See Mark 10:35–45.) "Even the Son of Man did not come to be served, but to serve, and to give his life as a ransom for many" (verse 45).

If you will lead your family, you must be willing to serve them. You must believe that their problems are your problems, their joys your joys, their needs your needs. When you do that, they will not owe you respect—you will have earned it, and they will gladly give it.

If you want to learn to put family first, study the actions and reactions of a puppy. Puppies have the five characteristics that "family first" leaders simply must learn to posses.

They Care about Your Presence, Not Your Past

Puppies are forgiving by nature. They don't ask where you've been, and they don't care what time you were supposed to be home. Whenever you arrive, they're glad to see you. Of course that doesn't nullify house rules or the setting of parameters for the safety of your children. It simply means that your family must understand that your home isn't complete without them.

Paul told New Testament Christians, "Be kind and compassionate to one another, forgiving each other, just as in Christ God forgave you" (Eph. 4:32). Like a puppy, cut people some slack. That's not a call to "cheap grace." It's a reminder that grace is great, and we all need it by the handful. Work to create a grace-filled home. Accept apologies, forget insults, and offer the most valuable gift imaginable: a second chance.

They Can't Hide Their Intentions

Puppies never fake their emotions. Their sloppy kisses, jump-up greetings, and wagging tails are always genuine. You never have to wonder what puppies are thinking—they act on every impulse that enters their mind.

Without being impulsive, you must be open and honest with your family. When you give praise, make sure it's genuine. When you have valid criticism or concerns, don't hold on to them; find appropriate and Christlike ways to make them known. All your goals must be out in the open; there are no hidden agendas. With a good leader, what you see is what you get.

They Don't Care about Your Pedigree

People are concerned with pedigrees, but puppies aren't. When the caregiver walks through the front door, a puppy never checks credentials or cares about the letters behind the name. Puppies know when they're loved, and that's enough.

You must major on caring. Dotting the i's and crossing the t's is never as important as ensuring the welfare of your family members. And always be more concerned with the souls of your family members than with their performance or their achievements.

They Are Loyal by Nature

Puppies will love you whether you feed them gourmet horsemeat from designer bowls or granulated bowwow biscuits on an aluminum plate. If there is a loyalty gene, all puppies have it.

Leaders in the home are loyal too. The greatest leader of all, Jesus, could have yanked the WWJD bracelet off the Apostle Peter's wrist after the fiasco around the campfire when Peter denied the Lord three times. Instead, Jesus forgave him and offered him a fresh ministry assignment: "Feed my sheep" (John 21:18).

Never give up on your family. Stick with them through the best and the worst.

They Are Enthusiastic

You can be sadder than a one-term governor on a two-year probation and still perk up when you see a puppy. Puppies have a way of spreading sunshine wherever they go. They enjoy life, and everybody knows it.

Good leaders love life, and that's not all. They love their work also. Their enthusiasm is contagious. They raise morale wherever they go. If you're turned on about leading your organization, your family won't tune out. Set a positive tone, and you'll get positive results.

Family first. That's the best advice any leader can receive. No home is stronger, wiser, or more dynamic than the people who comprise it. Build your family, and you'll build your future.

Sound impossible? If a puppy can do it, so can you!

21

CREATING AN ATMOSPHERE

OF AFFIRMATION

I once had a staff member who was very sensitive to the leading of the Holy Spirit when it came to compassionate ministry. As the leader of a hundred college students, he felt compelled to be their example of benevolence to the community, but he lost his balance along the way.

One day he confided in me. "I don't know what to do," he said. "I've been thinking seriously about selling my house and cars and taking my wife and kids to the streets to live among the homeless. I feel guilty ministering to them only occasionally, then coming home to the comfort and security of my home at night."

I looked at him and said, "You have a certain gift from God, and that is teaching. What your students need is someone to teach them how to minister to the homeless of our city, but not necessarily by moving to the streets. Your students need someone who will challenge their minds about the problems of the homeless and the methods they can use to meet them."

The relief registered on his face immediately. He simply needed someone to affirm his calling. It works in the home as well. As a leader, that is your responsibility for every member of your family. Celebrate their contribution. Show them the value of what they do. Your encouragement will help in keeping them on track in their personal life and in their spiritual life.

Palm trees don't grow in Alaska. It's too cold there. Tropical plants need warmth. Orchids don't bloom in the desert. It's too dry. Delicate flowers need plenty of moisture. If you want any plant to grow, you must provide the right atmosphere.

Obvious? Not always. Many leaders try to grow a family without providing the right climate. They need affirmation in order to thrive. Starve them for recognition and they'll dry up faster than a tiger lily in Tunisia. But give them plenty of encouragement and they'll grow as strong as sequoias and multiply like zucchini.

Here's how to create an atmosphere of affirmation in your home.

Celebrate Success

A family member has been working for weeks on a school or community project. She's exhausted herself, but the big push paid off. Her big day came off without a hitch. Now it's over, right? Not quite. As a leader in your home, you have one more job to do. Celebrate her success.

Never let an achievement slip by unnoticed. When minor objectives are reached, call attention to them. When major goals are accomplished, have a blow out. Throw a party, have dinner out, or give a reward. When your family succeeds, celebrate.

Praise in Private

Encourage your family members one-to-one. Tell them, "I appreciate you." Those "attaboy/girl!" ways will not only encourage them but also set an example for their encouraging others. Soon, you'll notice family members doing the same with others—and with you!

Praise in Public

Praise family members in front of others. Let them know how valuable your family members are in your eyes. Affirm your family in the hearing of others. Be fair and evenhanded, no playing favorites, and beware of arousing envy. Simply let each person in your family know how much you appreciate him or her as a person.

Pay Attention to Needs

Your praise will ring hollow if it's not grounded in reality. Saying, "You're doing a great job" may seem meaningless to one who believes he is struggling. But do it anyway. Keep connected. Observe their achievements—and failures—and offer encouragement accordingly. Asking, "How can we learn together from this?" can be just as affirming as praising a success.

Don't forget birthdays and anniversaries. Be there when family members are involved in a recreational, school, or community event—even if it means rescheduling an appointment or meeting. Show an interest in their hobbies. When family members know you're tuned in to their needs, they'll have a greater confidence in you.

Include Family

All of our compliments shouldn't be left at the church. Family members need those hugs of friendship and sympathy too. Cut them the same slack as you would a growing disciple in your discipleship class.

Bring a little sunshine into your home with the same intensity you would bring to a hospital room. I know that your home is a place where you can relax, but relaxing the common-sense actions of courtesy and kindness will do more harm than good.

Your family members believe in what you are doing. Give them the same positive reinforcement you'd give Sunday school teachers. Tell them their contribution matters.

Make Affirmation a Lifestyle

Are you an encourager? Some people aren't. Their pessimistic outlook on life spills into relationships. They dampen morale by dwelling on problems, never on praise.

Develop a personal style that promotes the success of others. Look family members in the eye and listen to what they say. Ask how they are and what they need. Frequently say things like "I love you," "thank you," and "good job." Your personal style will set the tone in your home.

Everyone thrives on encouragement. You are probably in a leadership position today because someone believed in you—and told you so. Remember how that affirmation motivated you, and practice it. Provide affirmation, and you'll help your family succeed.

22

POWER LISTENING

W e live in the age of the power lunch and the power walk. Why not power listening? What leaders learn about others may be just as important as what others learn from them. There will never be that transference of ideas without listening. But not just any listening— power listening. Extreme listening. The kind that gathers enough information from another to light visionary fires and provide warmth at the same time.

Leader, you must be that kind of listener. "Power listening" must be noted in the skills column of your résumé—and also in the hearts of your family members. It's that important!

You may be geared more to making sounds than absorbing them. Think of that toddler child who is quickest to squeal, yell, or talk. That's the child of whom it is usually said, "He's going to be a preacher, just like his daddy." But the greatest preachers have been those who had great listening skill. What they learned from others they translated into their greatest character qualities.

Become a power listener. James the apostle said it: "My dear brothers, take note of this: Everyone should be quick to listen" (James 1:19).

Here's a quick test of a leader's listening skill. Do you look into the eyes of the person speaking to you? If so, you are likely to be attentive, interested, and concerned about their needs. If not, you are probably distracted, unconcerned, or—worse yet—egotistical. Good leaders take people seriously. They pay attention to words, inflection, and emotion expressed by others—especially of those in their home.

Listen to Ideas

You may not act on every suggestion, but listen with an ear to hear fresh ideas. Understand that a concept that may propel you upward could very well come from someone in your home. Welcome suggestions from a spouse, a child, or other family members.

Leaders never arrive; they are always on a journey. Books line their path. Seminars are on their schedules. Conferences are on their checklists. But they will never learn enough to avoid listening. Wisdom is found in experiences as well as in night classes. There will be those who sit with you at the breakfast table who may have more common-sense insights about a church problem than a colleague with one or more seminary degrees.

You will work with some who don't have the foggiest how to map a flowchart. But a family member may have found a way around some pretty tall barriers—and learned about life from the first step to their present altitude. They may not be drawing Social Security. In fact, some of them won't be old enough to vote in the next election. God has a way of putting heavenly wisdom into earthly minds. He said that a little child shall lead.

Listen to Complaints

Emotions left unvented can become stifling at best, explosive at worst. Unresolved problems might very well suffocate family members. Value the feedback of your in-house critics.

The cries and concerns of others are cries for personal attention. Listen and understand that constant questions come from a heart that needs to know how to do what is right. Also understand that the complaints that are most irritating are often just.

Listen for what is unspoken. A problem may be present for some time before a family member has the courage to voice it as a complaint. Look for body language, expression, and other nonverbal clues to meaning. Like a well-trained mechanic evaluating the function of a racing engine, listen for the sounds that others miss.

Listen with Tomorrow in View

On a clear night, you can hear a train coming from a long way away. The sound is faint at first, almost imperceptible. But the trained ear can hear it. Listen for the train that has not yet arrived. Look for trends that are just over the horizon—trends that may be valuable or dangerous. Listen for changes in the economy that will affect the financial future of your family.

Leaders listen to those who have influenced other families. That speaker or author who has learned important principles for family living probably learned those principles on the job. Be open to new principles or methods for raising children or improving a marriage.

Be open to the advice of your peers.

Listen to young dreams and filter them through your own years of experience.

Become a power listener. Learn to listen, and you will learn to lead.

23

SAY GOOD-BYE TO BITTERNESS

Maybe you've heard the story of the old Oklahoma philosopher who was sitting on his porch when a man rode up in a frontier wagon and asked, "Hey, mister, is this town friendly?"

"Depends," the philosopher replied. "How was the town you came from?"

"Not friendly at all!" the pioneer announced. "That's why we left."

The wise old man responded, "Then you'll probably find this town about the same."

Later, an almost identical wagon filled with another pioneer family stopped and asked the same question.

"How was it where you came from?" the philosopher asked.

"Friendliest town we ever saw!"

The old man said, "You'll probably find this town to be the same."

Our attitude determines our experience in most areas of life. That's certainly true when it comes to experiencing joy. Those who look for it usually find it. Those who are convinced there is no joy to be had seldom seek it.

Have you ever had a family of giraffes over for dinner? Neither have I, but I can imagine what such an evening would be like. First, my wife would be scurrying around looking for a recipe for acacia-leaf casserole. Second, we'd have to put duct tape around the chandelier in the dining room. Then, we'd have to position the crystal water glasses on the floor beneath the table because giraffes are used to reaching down to take a drink.

The dining room chairs would have to be wired with reinforcements. We'd have to put a tarp over the houseplants so they wouldn't be eaten as appetizers. And you can only imagine how much fun it would be to clean up after such houseguests!

The more I think about it, I'll bet the only good thing about having giraffes over for dinner would be saying good-bye!

Harboring bitterness in the heart is a little bit like that. It makes our lives awkward. It wreaks havoc on our spirits. It causes us to say and do things we regret. It robs us of joy.

The only good thing to do with bitterness is to say good-bye to it. Here are three "giraffes" in the bitterness family, along with some ways to get rid of them.

Unforgiveness

Jesus emphasized the importance of forgiveness in clearing our relationships with God and others. And forgiveness has no limits. In response to Peter's famous question, "'How many times shall I forgive . . .? Up to seven times?' Jesus answered, 'I tell you, not seven times, but seventy-seven times'" (Matt. 18:21–22). In the Sermon on the Mount he added pointedly, "If you do not forgive men their sins, your Father will not forgive your sins" (6:15).

Who are the people from whom you need to ask forgiveness? Whom do you need to forgive? Don't allow unforgiveness to block the joy in your life or in your home.

Resentment

Seeds of healing won't grow in a heart of stone. To forgive means to give up or release. Jesus taught that mercy and love are at the core of genuine forgiveness. Neil Anderson said, "We must forgive in the same way we have been forgiven. In His mercy, God has given us what we need, not what we deserve."

These are people of whom you need to let go: the one who abused you as a child, those who have wounded you with their words, the one who took advantage of your generosity, the one who neglected you emotionally, and perhaps others known only to you.

Release feelings of resentment. It's the only way you will find healing.

Jesus said it, and I believe it: "When you stand praying, if you hold anything against anyone, forgive him, so that your Father in heaven may forgive you your sins" (Mark 11:25).

Anger

Anger is like a pair of muddy boots on a new carpet. It's heavy. It's messy. And the further it goes, the more enemies it makes. Sometimes our anger isn't obvious, even to ourselves. At other times it blossoms like a dandelion on a new lawn.

The accomplishments and adulations of those outside the home make our own setbacks more difficult to bear. If we dwell on them, they become festering sores.

Paul said, "Get rid of all bitterness, rage and anger . . . Be kind and compassionate to one another, forgiving each other, just as in Christ God forgave you" (Eph. 4:31–32).

Let go of anger before it takes hold of you. I don't propose to offer easy solutions to all of life's questions. Life is too complex for that. But I do know that if we settle some issues, our hearts are more settled and we have joy.

I look to Jesus as the only worthy model, and I see that He loved a world that hated Him; He stretched out His hands to those who pierced them with nails; He preached good news to those who doubted Him; He blessed those who cursed Him; and when they wounded Him, He prayed, "Father, forgive them."

Say good-bye to bitterness and you will welcome joy.

PART 3

MINISTRY

No amount of scholastic attainment, of able and profound exposition,
of brilliant and stirring eloquence can atone for the absence of a
deep impassioned sympathetic love for human souls.

—DAVID BRAINERD

I became a servant of this gospel by the gift of God's grace
given me through the working of his power.

—EPHESIANS 3:7

24

DELIVERING CONSISTENT PASTORAL CARE

When Dr. Billy Graham concluded his remarks at the national service of prayer and remembrance for the September 11 tragedy, the president of the United States, congressional and military leaders, representatives of the major religions, and the rest of the invitation-only audience rose to deliver a standing ovation. What a tribute to that esteemed preacher of the gospel who has become the nation's pastor! How we needed a pastor in those momentous days.

You may not receive that kind of recognition for your pastoral efforts, but to those who have been hurt or who grieve over the hurts of others, your pastoral care will be no less important. There will never be a substitute for your personal care of those in your congregation or organization. People need *you*. There will be times when they need you "in person." They will need your prayers. They will need that shared promise from God's Word.

Like brave rescue workers who fight fire and falling debris to rescue the injured or dying, you have committed yourself to climb into the rubble of this world and provide personal comfort. The commitment is not unlike the Master's: "The Spirit of the Lord is on me, because he has anointed me to preach good news to the poor. He has sent me to proclaim freedom for the prisoners and recovery of sight for the blind, to release the oppressed, to proclaim the year of the Lord's favor" (Luke 4:18–19).

Laypersons in your church must be an integral part of pastoral care. But some hands-on care is essential for every pastor. Here's a simple method for ministering personally to seven individuals in your congregation each day in a way that will bless you immensely and have a great impact on your congregation. I call it "ninety-minutes-a-day care." Here's how it works.

Spend One Hour in One-to-One Ministry

Take sixty minutes to encourage, build up, or praise someone whom you are seeking to influence. This can be done in your office, when that is most convenient or comfortable for the individual, but most often it is wise to do it outside the church walls. You won't want to spend this precious time conducting church business, and removing yourself from that setting eases the temptation. I like to take the person to a local restaurant for breakfast or lunch, and I always pick up the tab. The casual setting affords opportunity for both light conversation and meaningful dialogue, and if prayer seems appropriate, nobody minds. Most people love to have an interested party listen to them, so refrain from creating an agenda or talking about yourself as much as possible. Make this your guest's time to tell you what is on his or her mind and heart.

Of course, meeting someone of the opposite sex is not advised. In cases where the person's spouse is unavailable, arrange for your spouse to be present.

Spend Fifteen Minutes on Correspondence

Take fifteen minutes to send three brief notes, e-mails, or text messages to people within your sphere of influence. These could include birthday or anniversary cards, and you might invite volunteers (senior adults, perhaps) to address them. If you have staff members, they too can sign the cards. Unfortunately, when you have handwriting like mine, you'll want to have your church logo printed on your card so people will know where it came from!

Norman Vincent Peale said some years ago that "Christians ought to be in the business of building people up, because there are so many people today already in the demolition business." These notes should be directed by the four S's: sincere, short, specific, spontaneous.

Spend Fifteen Minutes on Phone Calls

The final dimension of this ninety-minutes-a-day care is spending fifteen minutes making brief phone calls to three people.

In my experience, this is best done systematically. Consider calling each church member on his or her birthday and anniversary. Keep a record of the calls so that you're sure to reach every person. You may wish to record the dates and telephone numbers in your PDA or cell phone. Also, a secretary or volunteer might assist you by writing each member's phone number in your pocket calendar on the appropriate day. For example, "Jeff Downs' B-day, 555-5689." Then, when you turn the page, the phone numbers are there for you. All you have to do is call and say, "Hi, Jeff. This is Pastor Goodguy. I want to wish you a happy birthday because I love you. I hope you have a great day!" If you have no birthday or anniversary calls, then make calls in alphabetical order, three a day, until you have spoken to every member during the year.

Crisis ministry is only part of the pastoral responsibility. Touching the lives of your people every day will build relationships, bless your people, and strengthen your church. Devoting ninety minutes each day to pastoral care makes the process feasible without exhausting the pastor.

The greatest pastor who ever lived knew the secret of caring for His people. Before He preached to them, He fed them. He is called the Great

Shepherd—and we may call Him the Great Example. During His earthly ministry, wherever people were in need, the Master made every attempt to minister to them.

Your sermon or lesson preparation is important. Your administration skills are vital. But your personal care for others will have the longest impact of your ministry.

25

ADDING DOORS TO YOUR CHURCH

I'm sorry, Pastor. We really love your preaching, but our family needs to be somewhere else right now."

Pastor Tim was shocked. Since his appointment to Epworth United Methodist two years ago, he'd bent over backward to be "all things to all people." He visited the nursing home twice a month and met with the church's few teenagers every Sunday night. He didn't have the time or the energy to add another ministry.

Dave continued. "It's our kids. They're six and nine, and we really don't have a ministry for them here. We need a church that has something for our whole family, so we're going to Southlawn."

Tim's heart sank as he fought back tears. *What more can I do?* he wondered.

Sound familiar? I know you've been there, struggling to attract and keep people, tiring yourself as you run in circles.

Here's an answer: Sunday school. This tried and true ministry has something for all ages. It's flexible, expandable, and highly dependable. If you don't have a Sunday school, start one. If you do have one, make it shine. This old standby can become your best friend!

"Look at all the people!" Lauren said. "Do they all belong to our church?" The multipurpose room was bustling with children and parents, young adults and seniors for Trinity Baptist's potluck dinner. Since the church added a third worship service in September, there were few occasions when the "whole family" got together.

"They sure do," Pastor Jane said excitedly.

"But where did they come from?" Lauren asked. "Adding a single worship service couldn't account for all this growth!"

"But we didn't add just one service," Pastor Jane said. "We added four."

"Four? I don't get it," Lauren replied.

"When we started the Saturday evening worship service, we also added three Christian education classes. Now, in addition to age-graded classes, we have a class for divorce recovery, one for new converts, and a class on understanding Christianity and Islam."

Lauren was astonished. "You mean people have started attending the church because of a class?"

"Why not?" The pastor smiled. "There's more to life than praise choruses, you know."

It's true. No single ministry of your church will reach everyone. Of course many people are attracted to the dynamic atmosphere of a vibrant worship service. But as Jane noted, people need more than energetic singing. And the weekend sermon alone can't fully equip the saint.

You need a variety of ministries that touch people at different levels. The more entrance points a church has, the more people it will attract. And Sunday school/small groups offer more entrance points than any other ministry. Here are some "doors" you can add to your church through Sunday school.

Age-Graded Doors

People like to be among others in a similar life stage. Sunday school naturally brings together teens with teens, young adults with young adults, and seniors with seniors. Adding an age-specific class adds an opportunity for growth.

Teaching Doors

Worship is a vital exercise for all believers. But Acts 2:42 reminds us that the apostles' teaching is another foundation stone of the Church. People are hungry for sound Bible teaching, and the Sunday school can provide it.

Fellowship Doors

The smaller the group, the greater the intimacy. Sunday school, with its naturally developed small groups, provides one of the best venues for fellowship in any church. Jesus taught the value of offering even a cup of cold water. Modern disciples have added the coffeepot. Lifelong friendships are formed in a Sunday school class. People looking for someone to care about their cares need a door of fellowship.

Special Interest Doors

When will Jesus return? What does the Bible say about other religions? Inquiring minds want to know. Vibrant Sunday schools are learning centers where important questions are answered in a friendly and informative way. Specialty classes offer a nonthreatening environment for those struggling with personal or social issues.

Lifestyle Doors

Massive changes in society may require similar changes in the local church. Who knows what's next! Three-and-a-half–day workweeks? What about the extended weekend? How will the church compete with the continuing growth of recreation? Sunday school is ideally suited to attract people based on lifestyle needs. It's flexible, expandable, and portable. It can accommodate groups of two to two hundred, on campus or off.

How many doors does your church have? How many ways do you have to mainstream people into your church ministry? The more the better!

How will you use the Sunday school to create new entry points to your congregation?

26

CONDUCTING THE
FUNERAL

Memorial services offer the pastor some of the most important ministry times in the entire church year. They are not only quality times for bringing comfort and encouragement to church families; they are times of building relationships with them and with their unchurched friends and families. They also offer the officiating minister an opportunity to express his or her compassion in the spirit of Jesus Christ. There are some important procedures that will heighten your ministry times. Some are familiar and others may not be as familiar.

From the moment you are notified of the death of a parishioner or parishioner's family member, your "intensive care" should be quite obvious. An *immediate* call on the family is highly important. That call will be as much about listening as it will be about offering advice, quoting Scripture, or saying prayers—though it may include all of that. Patient listening allows survivors to express their feelings.

Plans for the memorial service may be made during a subsequent call. The immediate call is an expression of sympathy on your behalf and on behalf of the church family.

Your words should be "seasoned with salt." Generally, expressions such as "God must have loved her so much He took her to be with Him" or "God trusts you enough to let this happen" should be avoided. No matter the lifespan of the deceased, the person's death still will bring sorrow and loss to the family—and to the extended family. The focus of your Scripture reading and prayer should be on love and concern for the family.

The family may or may not want you to conduct the funeral. If they have asked another pastor, don't be offended. Often arrangements have been made with a minister to conduct the funeral way before you were the family's pastor. Your understanding of their wishes—as well as your willingness to be available to participate if needed—expresses your spiritual maturity and love. If asked to conduct the service, a follow-up call will include the planning of a memorial service.

Assist the Family with Planning the Service

The family may want you to help them in making arrangements for the funeral. There may even be times when the family will want you to accompany them to the funeral home. Planning will include the location, date, and time of the service; graveside arrangements; and information about the funeral home. Additional information may be gathered from the survivors and recorded on a worksheet that includes the following:

Basic Information about the Deceased—full name (or nickname used), date of birth and birthplace, date of death and location, occupation, name of spouse, number and names of children and grandchildren, and other survivors.

Life-Centered Information—education, church affiliation, community service, hobbies/interests, awards/recognitions, and travel/adventures.

Funeral Services Information—viewing arrangements, officiating minister, assisting minister(s), favorite Scripture verse(s), favorite song(s), special music, musician(s) and accompanist's names, tribute(s), poems or readings, pallbearers, ushers (if necessary), sound (and recording, if requested), order of service, and requests of the deceased regarding their funeral.

Information about Memories and Relationships—personal family relationships, favorite memories, and humorous anecdotes.

Mobilize the Church

As pastor, you need not do all the pastoral care surrounding a funeral—but you will be the key person in activating that care. Every congregation should have a plan for surrounding a grieving family with love. Some key elements of that plan are these: sending flowers, organizing meals to be sent to the immediate survivors (spouse or children), offering a meal following the funeral service, offering to arrange transportation or housing (if necessary), and following up with other ministries, such as cards, visits, memorials, transportation, and so forth.

Plan the Memorial Service

Prepare a brief welcome and obituary, including naming immediate survivors. Choose brief opening Scripture verses (e.g., John 11:25). Include the reading of a song or a poem (perhaps a favorite of the deceased). Coordinate music selections with the musicians.

Also prepare your funeral sermon with these guidelines in mind: Make it scriptural, brief (ten to fifteen minutes), personal, and clear without being preachy (incorporate the salvation plan).

Prepare closing remarks and graveside or dinner announcements. Include a benediction (and committal service if necessary).

The Funeral

I have received calls from pastors conducting their first funeral, who asked about their role during the funeral service. Most often, that is learned by attending other funerals. But in case you're not familiar with the role of the pastor during a memorial service, let's go over some of the basics.

Prior to the Service. Check in with the funeral director to assure him or her of your presence. A private office may be offered for your preparation time. You may want to use that time to review your notes, and you may also want to use the time to pray for the surviving family and friends.

During the Service. You will lead the audience in honoring the life of the deceased from a platform area. On the advice of the funeral director, you may be asked to lead the procession of the casket to the front of the chapel or auditorium. You may want to express your respects by pausing with bowed head before the casket once it is in place. If it is a graveside service, you will stand at the head of the casket (the funeral director will inform you).

Generally, the sermon will be fifteen to twenty minutes in length. Your attitude will convey your respect for the survivors as well as the deceased. (A flippant attitude during the service suggests disrespect.)

Following the Service. You will lead the casket from the auditorium or chapel out to the waiting hearse. You may have an opportunity to greet the immediate family. At the graveside committal (which may include an opening Scripture reading, song or poem reading, benediction, and the committal), you will also have an opportunity to greet the immediate family, giving a lengthier time to greet them and assure them of your availability.

Of course, your ministry doesn't end with the memorial service. You will need to give ministerial care to the family for several weeks and months—making pastoral visits, writing notes of encouragement, and checking on them with a phone call. Also, I have written a letter of comfort on the first anniversary of the death of their loved one.

You represent the love of Christ at a crisis moment. And your loving concern may be just the thing to lead a friend or survivor into Christ's kingdom.

27

CONDUCTING THE WEDDING

Weddings are more than ceremonies. They are opportune times to develop relationships with the wedding party and friends. They are also times to share the gospel or encourage the couple in building a Christian home. Whether the couple are already members of the congregation or are seekers who come to your church because of their desire for a Christian wedding, the marriage ceremony is a prime opportunity for ministry. Here are several things that should be high on your list of duties.

Prepare the Couple

You should avoid officiating at weddings that haven't been preceded by a time of counseling. Premarital counseling is a key to the couple's understanding of marriage—and often key to understanding their roles as marriage partners.

If you are not comfortable in offering extended premarital counseling, you may want to enlist the help of a qualified professional. There is a wealth of premarital counseling material available—including books, DVDs, and seminars.

In your premarital counseling session, you will want to introduce the biblical context of marriage. You will also have an opportunity to share the principle of a Christian marriage, including a basic introduction of the plan of salvation and an assurance of your availability to minister to them throughout their marriage.

You may also want to assist the couple in choosing (or writing) their vows. Personalized wedding vows add much to the uniqueness of the service.

Prepare for and Execute the Ceremony

The wedding ceremony includes several key components.

Location. Your church may have a policy regarding the use of its facilities. The policy should be provided in written form and made available to the couple. It may include costs for use, custodial fees, statements about the use of tobacco and alcohol during the reception, and any restrictions regarding wedding reception activities.

You may want to refer the couple to your secretary for scheduling the facilities and for premarital counseling appointments. Make sure the details of dates and times for the counseling session(s), rehearsal, and wedding ceremony are carefully included (in the church calendar as well as in the pastor's planner).

Rehearsal. The wedding rehearsal is another key component of the wedding. You may offer suggestions to the couple regarding the ceremony—including a suggested order of service and rehearsal times. Once the rehearsal date and time are set, make sure the couple advises members of the wedding party to be on time for the rehearsal. At that time you will also want to inquire whether you (and your spouse) are expected to be a part of a rehearsal dinner.

A printed order of the wedding ceremony—including instructions for each member of the wedding party—will be of great help in insuring an orderly rehearsal. Generally, the pastor is in charge of the rehearsal.

You will want to assemble the wedding party for a time of prayer and an overview of the ceremony at the beginning of the rehearsal.

You (or a wedding planner) will instruct the wedding party about their entrances and exits, duties, and placement during the ceremony. (You may want to consider making a wedding planner available from your church. Their appointed service—which may include a fee paid by the couple—will relieve you of many details regarding the rehearsal and ceremony and will assist the couple with on-site direction for members of the wedding party.)

Make sure the wedding party is informed about meeting times for the wedding. (Late arrivals will add tension to the occasion.) And make sure you (or your appointed wedding planner) keep notes.

Ceremony. Be sure to be on time. You will want to have someone check to see that the lights have been turned on, that the heating or air conditioning has been adjusted, that dressing rooms for the wedding party are available, that the sound system is available, and that the musicians have everything they need for their performance *prior to their arrival.*

Be sure to check the facilities. You may want to designate someone to walk through the facilities to make sure that the rooms are in order— especially the restrooms and the nursery (if needed). Neatness and cleanliness add to the positive image of your church.

Be sure you have reviewed your notes. It's advisable that the couple's names be written into your copy of the wedding vows and to the introduction at the end of the ceremony. Any Scripture reading should be marked or written out.

Be sure to plan for emergencies. Members of the wedding party or the guests may fall ill—or faint. Instruct the ushers or wedding planner in reacting to the situation.

Candles may fall and ignite carpet or furniture. Build emergency plans into your preparation for the wedding.

Reception. Your presence (along with your spouse's) is an immediate goodwill gesture that projects the image of your church. Your friendliness to friends and family of the couple may be a bridge to their attendance at your church.

If the reception is held on-site, you (or your representative) may also be available to assist the caterers with information about the facilities and kitchen equipment.

Provide Ongoing Ministry

Often couples will tell you that they plan to come to your church after their return from their honeymoon. And often they fail to fulfill that promise. What can you do to assist them in fulfilling the promise?

First, make sure you've included the importance of church attendance in your premarital counseling.

Second, send a letter of congratulations and encouragement on church stationary as a follow-up. In that letter, you may want to invite them to attend the church and include a bulletin or a brochure that will inform them of service times and opportunities.

A small group or class on marriage may also be offered. Helping new couples adjust to their marriage is helpful not only in providing resources, but also in encouraging them to attend the church.

Pastor, whether you sense it or not, you are an important part of the wedding ceremony. Officiating with order and personal attention may result in a couple's dedication or rededication of themselves to the Lord.

28

PLANNING THE
WORSHIP SERVICE

I f the root word for *worship* suggests "worth-ship," then it only stands to reason that it should be worthwhile. The worth-ship of course is God directed. He is worthy of our best expressions of reflection and praise.

In one sense, the worship service should have a sense of spontaneity. You've heard the expression, "Lord, do something for us today that's not in the bulletin." But in another sense, it must be remembered that we serve a God of order, order that is seen everywhere in nature. Paul reflected that in his advice to those who were planning the worship services in Corinth: "Everything should be done in a fitting and orderly way" (1 Cor. 14:40).

How do you plan a worship service that gives glory to God, encourages and edifies the saints, and grabs the attention of visiting guests—all at the same time?

Begin with Prayer

Each worship service should have a heavenly design. Whether planning a Saturday evening seeker service or a Sunday morning traditional, the worship team should seek the mind of the Lord in planning the direction of the service. Times of prayer, reading of Scriptures, and sensing the direction of the Holy Spirit in meeting the needs of the congregation should be a priority.

Consider the Flow

The kind of worship service that reflects careful planning has a good flow. Parishioners, like their nonparishioner friends, are used to "entertainment" increments of thirty to sixty minutes. Why? They're TV watchers, part of the culture that spends an average of forty-four hours per week in front of electronic boxes that transmit high-definition signals and low-definition messages!

Great gaps in the worship service—while a microphone battery is changed, a musician is trying to find his or her place in a music score, or while the platform personnel are trying to decide who or what is next—is not the best image for your service and will not hold the attention of the TV culture.

A careful checklist of worship details will help you avoid a lot of "gospel gaffes."

- Is there a printed order of service for every participant?
- Have the microphone batteries been changed?
- Has the lighting been checked?
- Is the PowerPoint presentation in order?
- Have the musicians done a sound check?
- Is the accompaniment CD cued?

You should also think about the mood of the service. What atmosphere are you trying to create? Quiet or boisterous? Reflective or revival?

You may begin setting the worship "mood" during the pre-service. For example, pre-service music should be carefully planned. (Granted, sometimes the pre-service time becomes a shouting contest between the musicians trying to give directions over the volume of the praise band and parishioners trying to catch up on the latest gossip.)

A special song, dramatic reading or skit, a PowerPoint or video roll-in can help to create emotional and spiritual anticipation for worship—and quiet the chatter.

Also, sensitivity to the worship *moment* creates greater flow. For example, a spiritual Kodak moment shouldn't be followed by silliness. That awesome breakthrough just might be a bridge to another. The unusual presence of the Spirit, a spontaneous and spirited testimony, or a heartwarming reaction to a special song may be time for a "pause" rather than a "fast forward."

Remember the Platform-to-People Principle

There's an interesting theory of ministry: The more people in the program, the more people in the audience. Simply, the more people you can incorporate into the worship program, the greater the attendance. Think about those high attendance days. When do they usually happen? When the children's choir is on the platform. On the awards and recognition Sunday. On the night of the dramatic presentation.

Extra folks on the platform usually mean extra folks in the pews.

Continually Improve Execution

Praise teams have become a prominent fixture in most worship services. Some teams improve the worship experience, while others impede it. A sloppily attired, ill-trained, or untalented praise team can result in a long-lasting negative impression.

The difference lies in several factors.

Worship Team Members Should Be Enlisted. Auditions or not, praise team members should have obvious abilities—and an obvious spirit of ministry.

Worship Team Members Should Be Instructed. Leading worship is more than just singing. It involves appropriate attire, good platform presence, good eye contact, and an enthusiastic spirit.

Worship Team Members Should Be Encouraged. Much of what the team will hear is criticism. They need an encourager—someone who will recognize their efforts.

Improve Announcements

The method and manner of giving calendar and program announcements can also add quality to your worship service. Modern technology will never replace the bulletin, but it can be used in tandem, and actually enhance it. PowerPoint announcements on the overhead screen or TV monitors in hallways can effectively give attendees much needed information about your church services.

Announcements from the pulpit deserve careful consideration. First, they should be given by someone who has spiritual credibility, a good platform presence, and is able to read effectively. It isn't necessary to read the entire bulletin to the congregation. They probably have one in hand. Reading it word for word only suggests that they aren't able to read for themselves. Only the most pressing bulletin highlights should be shared.

A short, well-rehearsed, and appropriate skit may give attention to an important upcoming event. Also, video roll-ins may often be secured without charge from the organization whose event you are hosting and promoting.

Multiplied millions of dollars are spent on media commercials. Technique and attractiveness get the message across. The local church could learn a lot about promoting its program and personnel by taking a few tips from the pros.

29

EXTENDING YOUR INFLUENCE

M uch of your church's reputation rides on your own. If you are known in the community as a leader and an engaging people person, you'll attract others to your church—and to the gospel. Remain aloof, and they will too. Pastor, consider yourself God's man or woman in your community. You are an ambassador of the kingdom of God. Your credentials were given to you at your ordination, but your mission may have begun long before.

John Wesley said, "The world is my parish." If that was true for him, then our neighborhood, city, and county must be our parish also. It's a mistake for pastors to concentrate all their energy within the church walls. The world is our mission. Here are some tips for extending your influence beyond the church doors.

Improve the Image of Your Church

Many people will form an opinion of your church—and your leadership—behind a steering wheel. They'll get their first impression while driving by your church, and that impression will last. If your facilities look run down or out of date, they'll figure that your congregation is too.

Improving your image can be done in the simplest ways. A fresh coat of paint works wonders for any building. Be sure that someone mows the grass and trims the shrubbery. See to it that signs are well placed and well lit. Plow the parking lot when it snows. Watch for cracks in the cement steps. If the building looks good, you do too.

Use Local Media to Get Your Message Out

You don't have to live in a large city to have interactions with the news media. Nearly every town has at least one newspaper, even if it's a free shopper. Radio stations dot the landscape, and everybody has access to TV and the Internet. What you may not realize is that local news producers are always looking for content and are often willing to run news items or feature stories about events at your church. The media has a Web page, column, time slot, or public access commitment to fill. Why not fill it with news about your church?

Compile a list of local media contacts and learn their submission guidelines. Get in the habit of sending news releases at least two weeks ahead of any major event at your church. You'll get into the paper, and you might just make the evening news. That publicity is worth a fortune in extending your message and your influence in the community.

Cooperate with Colleagues

When one pastor says something, it's not news. When several pastors join together to feed the hungry, fight homelessness, or promote an event, people notice. Cultivate relationships with your colleagues and work together whenever possible. It's true that you won't have much in common with some of them. But you all believe in Christ, and you will raise your collective profile by working together. Lone rangers are not the real heroes. Work as a team whenever you can.

Join Community Organizations

From civic clubs to the library board to fire departments, there are lots of volunteer organizations that are working to better your community. Help them when you can. You'll meet community leaders and gain their respect. You'll keep in touch with what's happening, raise the profile of your congregation, and you just might win key leaders for the gospel! Volunteer as a police chaplain. Serve on the community relations committee at the hospital. Your service on the board of a local agency may be the sermon about Christ's compassion that someone has been waiting to hear.

Get involved in the world around you. Christ was moved by the needs of those around Him, and He responded with a word, a touch, or a spirit of compassion. Modeling His concern in your community will go a long way in extending your influence.

Preach the Gospel Not Politics

A word of caution is needed here. Some pastors go overboard on their involvement with the community, becoming better known for advocating political or social causes than the gospel. Advocate life, feed the hungry, and educate children, but never allow your political concerns to dilute your effectiveness as a pastor. When you are invited to speak at a community event, use the occasion to present Christ, not the cause of the day.

Don't let your influence stop at the edge of the parking lot. You're a leader in the church; that makes you a leader in the community. Rise to the challenge! Enlarge your influence for the sake of the gospel.

30

ENSURING A
SECOND VISIT

Every church gets some visitors, but not all visitors return. How can you ensure that those who try your church one time will be eager to try it twice? Ushers and greeters are prime-time players in making people feel welcome in your church. From greeting new visitors and regular attendees, to helping those with special needs, to receiving the offering, to dealing with emergency situations, your ushers and greeters are an extension of the pastoral team. But "ambassadorship" often needs improvement.

There are some important questions that you may want to ask in evaluating and upgrading your ushering and greeting ministry.

Is It Organized?

Choosing persons who are dependable, outgoing, spiritually mature, and gifted in leadership to organize your welcome and assistance program is crucial to the image making of your church.

Calling ushers out of the audience to receive the offering, or a spur-of-the-moment hand-off of bulletins to someone standing by the entrance door may get an immediate job done, but the long-range effect will result in sloppy service.

Your ushering and greeting team, appointed by the pastoral team, may consist of the following: (1) a chairperson, who will provide over-all direction to the committee; (2) a head usher or head greeter who will recruit, train, assign, monitor, and encourage their staff; and (3) a safety director, who will be responsible for the overall protection of the worshipers and their personal belongings prior to, during, and following the scheduled services—including parking and emergency assistance.

Is There a Job Description?

Your welcoming team should know exactly what you expect of them. The job description may include the following:

Mission and Purpose. Ushers and greeter personnel should know that their service includes more than passing offering plates, setting up chairs, shaking hands, or parking cars. Their task is to provide a communications bridge.

Specific Duties. Each member of the team should know *where* they should be before, during, or following the services; *when* they should be at their appointed place; and *what* they should be doing to make people feel safe, comfortable, welcome, and ready for instruction or worship.

Scheduling and Substitution. Team members should be instructed in carrying out their assignments as scheduled. And they should know the team's policy regarding substitution in case of absenteeism.

Dealing with Emergencies. Team members should know the policy for dealing with emergencies: Where to find posted emergency telephone numbers or evacuation plans, location of equipment, a list of emergency personnel who may be in attendance, the protocol for contacting the pastoral team, reporting incidents, and transporting or immobilizing victims.

Dealing with Disturbances. Usher and greeter job descriptions could also include instructions and policy for dealing with disturbances (interruption of class time or worship service, parking lot disturbance, thefts, or threats). Team members should know *who* to contact, *how* to deal with specific disturbances, and *what* reporting procedures should be followed.

Seating Protocol. Job descriptions should include policy for seating worship attendees before and during church services. They should be instructed to seat people only during certain intervals—not to seat guests during specific times of the worship service (e.g., prayer, special song, offering, and so forth).

Have Ushers and Greeters Been Trained?

Efficient ushering and greeting ministries are dependent on good training. Training may be conducted in a one-day seminar, during the Christian education time, or in extended, weekly sessions (four to six weeks).

The training may include mission and purpose, procedures and policies, emergency training (CPR, basic first aid), tour of the facilities (to locate emergency equipment, and so forth), evacuation drills, and drills in dealing with disturbances and emergencies.

Training times also provide opportunities for building team morale, for teaching spiritual principles (spiritual gifts and so forth), and for promoting cooperation, and may be an ideal place for interaction with the pastoral team.

Training may also include informal times (with light refreshments or a meal).

Do Ushers and Greeters Go the Extra Mile?

Whether it's a five-star hotel or a popular restaurant, it's the extra touches that keep people coming back: a friendly atmosphere, a warm welcome, quick assistance, helpful information, good signage, valet parking, and continual attention. Your church can provide its own extra touches: parking lot greeters (with umbrellas handy), information and escort to nursery and childcare areas, handy and attractive bulletins and brochures on hand, assistance for people who have special needs (e.g., providing handicapped parking, ramps and seating areas for wheelchairs, providing information about deaf ministries, hearing assistance, and so forth).

Do Ushers and Greeters Provide Helpful Information?

Ushers and greeters can also assist in your ministry by gathering of helpful follow-up information: assisting with the welcome center, distributing attendance folders or visitor cards, inviting visiting guests to sign guest books.

Lobby or parking lot greetings may also be helpful in discovering first-time guests, visiting dignitaries, or people with special needs. Ushers and greeters can gather visitor information for use by the office staff in sending welcome letters.

Additionally, lobby or parking lot greeters may discover such information as hospitalizations, deaths, or special honors. Information gained from the friendly greetings (and friendships) of the ushers and greeters can be given to the pastoral staff for follow-up ministry.

Do You Emphasize Order?

The way in which your ushers and greeters serve may be even more important than how long they serve. Even their positioning in the auditorium conveys organization and orderliness. Ushers and greeters should also be trained to spend their time talking to arriving and parting parishioners, rather than talking among themselves.

Do You Praise Ushers and Greeters in Public and in Private?

Ushers and greeters often receive little or no attention. Their faithfulness should be recognized in public announcements, in church publications, and in notes or letters of appreciation. Milestones (years of service) can be recognized with a certificate, wall plaque, gift card, or some other honor.

Recognition of team efforts heightens team morale and propels team members to excellence. If you really think about it, you can provide a heavenly welcome to your visitors and regular attendees!

Your church image is often as good as its greeting.

31

LEADING A
WORSHIP TEAM

I t happens every week.

Sometimes the effect is grand and dramatic, like the crashing of a cymbal. At other times, it's subtle, almost invisible, like the rising of the tide. Every week we gather together for fellowship, teaching, the breaking of bread, and prayer, and every week it happens. God comes to meet with us.

Weekly worship is the high point in the life of the Church. It is the time when we gather to celebrate who Christ is and who we are in Him. Our service ministries are useful. Our outreach ministries are vital. Our compassion ministries are essential. But none of them would happen without the power that we gain by meeting together in the presence of God. We need to worship.

Pastor, you are the worship leader in your congregation. You set the tone for each weekly gathering. You lead the people by word and example before the throne of grace. Your knee is the first one bowed before God, and you are last to rise. This vital ministry depends on your leadership and spiritual integrity.

When I began my ministry, the worship team included the organist, the pianist, and me. Times have changed! Today even smaller or midsized churches may include several musicians, vocalists, and other participants in worship. And drama ministries are often used to complement the pastor's message.

These are good changes. They show that churches are taking worship seriously, and more people are involved in planning and leading this vital ministry.

These innovations have a price, however. They require a greater investment of time from both the laity and the pastor. Your plate is already full; will you have time to add a worship rehearsal and a drama practice every week?

You shouldn't have to. Here's how to direct a vibrant worship program without adding another evening to your week.

Make Worship the Goal

When you recruit people to serve in the worship service, be sure they know the goal: to assist the congregation in exalting Jesus Christ. When you gather your team for any reason, state that purpose again. Tell it to the congregation. Let every person who enters your church on the weekend know the reason you are there. Remind yourself of that purpose every time you prepare to preach. Set the top note for worship, and your worship team will harmonize with you.

Define the Team Broadly

"Worship" is sometimes used as a synonym for "music." It's not. Worship includes everything we do together that glorifies God. That means that the worship team includes more than the musicians who lead the congregation in singing. Everyone who is involved in the planning and execution of your weekend services is a part of your worship team. Get them all on board.

Set the Agenda

Get alone with God, hear what He has to say, and then tell others. That's the essence of worship leadership. When you understand the goal for each week's worship and communicate it to your team, you'll have a vibrant worship gathering.

Do you plan to present the gospel? Be sure your prayer team knows that. Do you intend to exalt God the Father? Let your musicians know. From greeters to communion stewards to drama team members, everyone who takes part in leading the service should know your goal. When they do, they will help you reach it.

Give Your Job Away

What roles do you play in worship, other than preaching? Do you select the music? Prepare communion? Make announcements? Read Scripture? Fold bulletins? Each of those things can be done by someone else. When you give your job away, you'll have more time to concentrate on ministry of the Word and prayer, and you'll gain broader participation in the church's worship life. Recruit well, set expectations, and follow-up. Be the leader, not the team.

Create Spiritual Checkpoints

You've lived this nightmare. The soloist gives a longwinded speech that has nothing to do with the worship service. The lay reader shows up late and can't remember what Scripture he or she was supposed to read. Meanwhile, the keyboard player and the guitarist are feuding over who sets the tempo for the songs. You don't know whether to blow a gasket or hide under the pew.

Worship leadership involves people in the church's most exciting and most technical experiences—all in full view of the congregation. It's no wonder that egos, emotions, and even tempers sometimes show. You can avert that by building spiritual checkpoints into your team's life. Insist that every subteam spend time in prayer when they practice or rehearse. Meet with your team leaders periodically for a spiritual checkup and accountability time. Ask, "How's the morale on your team right now? What can I do to help your team members stay focused on the goal of exalting Christ?"

Celebrate Together

The worship service should be the high point of your church's life and the life of each member. If done well, worship leadership will help your people experience God. That's exciting! Let your team know how important they are. Remind them of the eternal value of what they're doing. Celebrate every success and quickly move beyond any failure.

Every Sunday, we meet together, and God meets with us. Lives are changed right under our very noses. As pastors, it's our privilege not only to take part in this miracle but also to lead it. Lead well. Lives depend on the result.

32

INSPIRING CONFIDENCE

O n my first day at the office of my new pastorate, I received a visit from a church leader. "Welcome, Pastor," he said with a smile. "We're glad you're here!" Then he added this cryptic comment: "You sure have your work cut out for you." Did I ever!

The church had recently been divided by a bitter feud. When the prior pastor left, so did one-third of the people. Those who remained were angry, hurting, and filled with pessimism.

The future certainly looked bleak. But it wasn't. We rallied from that low point in the church's history to reach even greater heights than before. Old wounds were healed, and the people became filled with optimism instead of despair. In the process I discovered that it is possible to lead with hope—to help people discover the possibility of overcoming a painful past and looking toward a bright future.

Here are some of the tactics I used in order to bring both healing and hope to my new congregation.

Remember What's Good

Many churches struggle or die because they don't have a vision. They are without hope. And every church's vision begins with its history. Each congregation has a story to tell. Before the future can be seen clearly, the past must be understood fully. One of my early projects at the new church was to write its seventy-five-year history. We included anecdotes, statistics, highlights, photographs, and testimonials. It provided the foundation for all that followed in our mission.

Whether your church's history is positive or painful—and it's probably both!—you must understand its past in order to plan for its future.

Involve Leaders

Once the foundation of the past was formed, a vision for the future began to be communicated. Through preaching and teaching on the positive and powerful directions of the Lord, the church and its leadership began to see a new direction. Developing the church's vision—and thus developing hope—begins with the church leaders. In today's skeptical society, you cannot simply walk to the pulpit and say, "I've heard from God, and this is the way it's going to be." You might hear someone shout back, "I heard from God, too, preacher, and that's not what He said to me!" If you want to develop a vision that will be caught by everyone, it must first be caught by the leaders.

Let your leadership team fine-tune the future. Prayerfully guide in an evaluation of its present characteristic; then let them "dream about the future." Guide them in outlining the steps that will be necessary for its ministry success. This may be done in a daylong session, in a series of meetings, or in a retreat setting.

You plant the seed of hope. Then let it germinate in a setting of open discussion. The result will be a harvest of hope.

Focus on Others

Leading people with hope always has a mission in mind. And according to the gospel, that mission includes ministry to people. Your church isn't just about property or staff or program; it's about people. Your church's vision for the future must always include focusing on the needs of others. Being aware—and then creating awareness in the congregation—of the needs in your community is vital to developing a visionary plan to meet those needs. A local church that only reaches inward will become more of a repair shop than a hospital.

I'll never forget one board meeting where we brainstormed ideas for reaching our community. One person said, "You know what I think our church needs? Flowers." *Flowers?* I thought. *Give me a break!* But I allowed the person to state the idea fully.

"This is one of the busiest intersections in the city," the board member continued. "Each day about sixty-five thousand cars pass by our church. We look like just another office building. We have poor signage, and there's nothing that says welcome to the people who drive by. We need flowers to call their attention to us and to make them feel welcome."

The next day, this man put his money where his mouth was. He not only sent his personal gardener to landscape the church grounds, but handed me a check for three thousand dollars as well. Today when you pull up to that facility, the view is breathtaking. Passersby have actually turned into the driveway just to take pictures of the flowers!

By focusing on people instead of problems the leadership team developed a vision—and began to think with hope instead of hurt.

Include Biblical Priorities

To lead with hope you must always use the Bible as a road map. Your vision must include the priorities that are already established in the Word of God. The goals and strategies drawn up by the leadership team should always be linked to biblical priorities, including such things as evangelism, discipleship, stewardship development, and church planting.

The Bible is a book of hope. Every book of the Bible leads to the last one—the one where Christ returns in power and glory to set up His kingdom on earth. Communicate the biblical foundation for your vision in every way you can: Preach about it at least annually, include it in your church reports, and weave it throughout your church publications. Remind people that what you are doing is based soundly on the Word of God. And the Word of God is a Word of hope.

It is possible to rally from defeat. Your future endeavors can be even brighter than your past triumphs. All that is needed is a leader with hope and a vision—a leader like you.

33

EFFECTIVE EVANGELISM

There still is only one way to heaven (John 14:6).

You are a preacher and teacher of that way. You were appointed to preach and teach the gospel, the good news that God loved the world enough to sacrifice His only Son for their salvation. It should be at the very core of your ministry—the primary mission of your church— and the underlying theme of its every message or lesson.

You were appointed to tell people how they can get to heaven from where they are. Knowing how to do that effectively should be one of your chief goals! And knowing how to teach others to do that should be a high priority for your ministry.

There are a multitude of ways to share the plan of salvation. But many of them simply aren't being utilized. You can make a difference in that trend. You can teach your parishioners by example and by training how to lead another person to Christ.

Soul winning is still a "front burner" item. The church has many goals, but it only has one primary purpose: to share the saving and sanctifying work of Christ with as many people as possible. How do you communicate the purpose to your congregation? How do you make it the core of its ministry?

Know It Personally

I know of gospel preachers and teachers who know the gospel but have never experienced the gospel. Maybe they saw vocational ministry as a way of using their skills as a speaker or administrator. Maybe they just climbed the educational ladder, graduating from a Christian college or seminary into ordination, without ever having a born-again experience.

Priority number one is a personal and growing relationship with Christ through faith in His atoning work. You cannot share what you have not experienced. The Apostle Paul had that background. He was from a religious family, was schooled in the finest schools, and worked diligently to promote his religion. But he didn't know Christ—until that day on the road to Damascus, when his life was changed. After that the gospel was not a secondhand experience. Ephesians 3:7 reads, "I became a servant of this gospel by the gift of God's grace given me through the working of his power."

Include It in the Message

Paul explained, "Now, brothers, I want to remind you of the gospel I preached to you, which you received and on which you have taken your stand" (1 Cor. 15:1). The message of the gospel should be a continuing theme in your preaching schedule. In fact, the basic ABC principles—**A,** Admit you are a sinner, based on Romans 3:23 ("For all have sinned and fall short of the glory of God"); **B,** Believe that Jesus Christ died for you, based on John 1:12 ("Yet to all who received him, to those who believed in his name, he gave the right to become children of God"); **C,** Confess that Jesus Christ is Lord of your life, based on Romans 10:9–10 ("That if you confess with your mouth, 'Jesus is Lord,' and believe in your heart that God raised him from the dead, you will be saved. For it is with your heart that you believe and are justified, and it is with your mouth that you confess and are saved")—can easily be sown into your message.

Include It in Programming

A presentation of the principles of the gospel can be included in ministry at every age level. For example, one segment of your pastor's class or membership class may include the presentation. Your children's church ministry may include a "Decision Sunday," where the message of the gospel is presented. Video and DVD testimonials by Christian sports personalities may be presented during your weekly youth program.

Small group studies are an ideal place for presenting the gospel. Women's or men's groups, for example, may include a Bible study on knowing God or how to share your faith.

Highlight It in Church Property

Signage in the front lawn, the foyer, classrooms, fellowship centers, and in the worship center should include verses that speak of the gospel. Visitors may be presented with the basic principles of the gospel even before they reach the worship center. Anywhere people linger or stop is a good place to include attractive signage that highlights the gospel message.

Focus on It Periodically

Not only can the presentation of the gospel be a running theme in the preaching, teaching, and small group ministries of the church, other opportunities to hear its message arise in the form of an evangelistic crusade or rally. Participate in planning the event, advertise the event in your church publications and media presentations, and organize a church-wide effort—including transportation—to have a delegation from your church. And make the rally a part of your prayer emphasis.

Present It Individually

Every member of your leadership or teaching team should be taught how to share the gospel. Weekly, monthly, or yearly training sessions will equip your team in sharing the plan of salvation and in new believer follow-up.

On the road to Gaza during New Testament times, the disciple Philip encountered a man who was reading from the Old Testament prophecies in his chariot. His actions and the man's reactions are stirring reminders to all of us about the need for presenting the gospel: "Then Philip ran up to the chariot and heard the man reading Isaiah the prophet. 'Do you understand what you are reading?' Philip asked. 'How can I,' he said, 'unless someone explains it to me?' So he invited Philip to come up and sit with him" (Acts 8:30–31).

There is someone on every road of life that needs someone to explain how their sorrow can be turned to joy. A vision that begins in your heart may end up in the heart of that person!

34

IMPROVING YOUR PRINT IMAGE

Some of the most helpful and practical information in the Bible was sent in letter form. The quality of your correspondence directly affects the communication of your information. Quality is important. Let's look at a few areas of church correspondence that certainly deserve quality control.

Business and Information Correspondence

The formal letters of your church should be just that: formal. Correspondence from your church to governmental agencies, community organizations, or businesses should represent the best of your local church ministry. Also, legal or organizational correspondence to your parishioners should reflect the dignity and importance of your church. So, a few reminders are in order.

Use Quality Letterhead and Layout. Your church logo may be the focal point of your church letterhead. It should have some other characteristics as well: It should be uncluttered (limit, one cross to a page!); it should contain all of the basic contact information (name, address, telephone, fax, e-mail, Web site address, staff information); its color should be in dignified hues rather than gaudy; it should have a professional look. The body of the letter should have a standard business-letter feel—never italicized or written with an unusual font.

Create Quality Content. Often you can go to a letter template in your word processing program and just "plug and play" your message into an already formatted letter. Note: *Never* send a handwritten piece of correspondence as a business letter. In addition, run a spell check, carefully craft sentences and paragraphs, be brief, be clear, and include an appropriate salutation and closing.

Offer a Quality Presentation. Of course, your letterhead and your envelope should match. A good letter can be ruined with a sloppy mailing package. A postage meter adds a nice touch, but if that isn't in your budget, be sure your stamps have a professional look (for example, avoid "Elvis Anniversary" or "Looney Toons Legends"), are carefully positioned on the envelope, and are in the right amount.

Second, your letters should be timely. The timeliness with which you issue or answer business or informational correspondence says volumes about you and about your church. Business or organizational correspondence deserves immediate attention. Even well-formatted letters with good content will have a negative impact if not delivered in a timely fashion. (A rule of thumb might be a twenty-four- to forty-eight-hour response time.) Parishioner correspondence should also be delivered in a timely manner. (For example, membership letters, inquiry letters, or congratulatory letters should be mailed ASAP.)

Third, your letters should be positive. Friendly, Christlike correspondence will have a positive effect on its recipients. Even when negative items need to be addressed, they should be said in such a way that reflects positively on the church and the Kingdom.

Fourth, your correspondence should be archived. A secure file (computer file with a hard copy backup) of your business and informational letters should be kept indefinitely. Not only are those letters used for referencing, they may also be used as "exhibits" in any legal actions.

Guest Correspondence

Nothing says "Welcome!" like a welcome letter. Your visitor may have whisked by the greeter, so warm, friendly, and personal welcome letters say, "You really do matter to this church."

Church Letterhead. Corresponding with visitors on a church letterhead is a more "formal welcome" but it does have some positives. It gives wider information. The letterhead automatically gives the basic contact information about the church and its pastoral staff (and can be enhanced by an enclosed brochure—which probably fits into a #10 business envelope).

Note Card. Desktop publishing also makes it possible to welcome visitors with a tent card. Using a template, your church logo and address can be placed on packaged note cards and envelopes. The inside copy may either be neatly handwritten by a volunteer (chosen carefully), or a handwriting font may be used.

Postcard. Digital photography combined with desktop publishing makes it possible to create personalized postcards that feature a defining personal or property photo. The message copy from the pastor can be warm and brief and merged with an address file.

E-mail. If there is an e-mail option on your visitor card, you can give an immediate and effective welcome electronically. The message can either be delivered on an HTML file (perhaps duplicating the church letterhead) or can be put into a Rich Text file (using a formatted heading that includes date, church name, pastor information, salutation, copy, and signature).

Appeal Correspondence

Your annual stewardship emphasis or capital campaigns can be highlighted in an effective all-church mailing.

Design a Theme Letterhead. Include the logo and theme statements on letterhead that has a matching envelope. A neat, uncluttered, well-designed letter with a reader-friendly typeface and warm colors can be an immediate communication bridge to your congregation.

Put a Short "Teaser" on the Envelope. You have less than five seconds to grab the attention of the person who picks up the mail. A brief identifying or eye-catching sentence puts you at the advantage.

Start with a Story. Personal anecdotes or references draw the reader in to the copy of the appeal letter. A statement, testimonial, or story gives the reader a point of reference, and it gives the letter a warmer feel.

Plan the Communication Path. After the opening, the most important information about the appeal should follow. The who, what, when, where, and why of the appeal needs to be clearly stated.

Add a Postscript. Often, the most important copy (and most often read) is in the postscript. Putting a summary of the letter copy, or added information, into a brief sentence that follows the signature is highly effective. You may also want to include a response time (emphasizing dates and goals).

You have a wonderful opportunity to project quality in various correspondence: membership welcome letters, baptism follow-up, infant dedication, graduate recognition, job promotions, and community service recognition.

Compile your letters prayerfully, carefully, and positively. Quality counts.

35

TEN TIPS FOR

HOSPITAL VISITATION

Hospital visitation isn't an option for growing churches. It can be covered by a staff member or layperson, but pastors should be directly involved. Having served large churches during my pastoral career, I am quite aware that doing hospital visitation can become quite challenging as the church grows larger. It is my view that the senior pastor should become the facilitator of pastoral care and train key leaders who have the gift of mercy. Also, many times large churches are able to hire pastoral staff to assist in the process.

Some of your greatest relationships will be formed during a medical crisis. Pastor, you need to be visible when members of your congregation—or their family members—are hospitalized. Here are some tips for hospital visitation.

Become Familiar with Hospital Policy

Know the visitation policy of the hospital you plan to visit. What is its policy regarding clergy visitation? What identification is needed? Is there a designated parking area? What restrictions are in place regarding visitation times? Are there areas that hospital personnel consider off-limits to clergy? Your cooperative spirit will build lasting impressions of your ministry—and of your church.

A forceful or belligerent attitude may hinder the option of future visits, negatively influence the attitude of the hospital personnel or the patient's opinions about the Kingdom, and cause division between other clergy and you.

One way to bridge the ministry-hospital personnel gap is to volunteer. Be available for chaplaincy duties if possible. Serve in hospital fund-raising ventures. Honor the medical staff in a community service award ceremony during a worship service. Goodwill always goes a long way.

Know the Patient

Know as much about the patient and the patient's reason for hospitalization as possible. Without prying, gaining knowledge of their affliction or condition may prevent foot-in-mouth disease. Learning about the patient's hobbies or interests may be a good conversation builder during the visit.

Visit at Appropriate Times

Some hospitals will allow clergy unlimited visitation. Others will prefer clergy visitation at designated times—and in designated areas. As much as possible, your visits should be during times that will be convenient for the patient and for the hospital personnel. For example, patient bathing, patient testing, patient therapy, change of dressings, or room cleaning usually takes place during the morning hours.

Most hospitals will allow presurgery visits by clergy at any time. Even then, the pastor should be alert to the surgical patient's preparation for surgery. Pastors should be present for major surgeries—but should not get in the way of staff procedures.

Also, visiting clergy should guard themselves by making appropriate visits to children or youth. Make sure someone else knows you are there—and why you are there. In those cases, it would be best to make visits when family members are present.

Dress Appropriately

You not only represent your local church, you represent the Kingdom when you make a hospital visit. Clergy who look (or smell) like they've just run a 5K race or came directly from the gym may do more harm than good! Dress-up or casual is your call, but make sure appropriateness, cleanliness, and neatness reign.

Focus on the Patient

You are there to see the patient. Focus on that patient. Of course, you'll be friendly to family, friends, or hospital personnel, but be sure that the patient doesn't feel left out of the conversation (unless they are unconscious or sleeping). The patient wants to know you are listening to his or her concerns. That process will include listening to complaints as well as compliments—without agreeing or disagreeing with them.

Hospital visits shouldn't be a time for church business. Your hospitalized parishioners are more concerned about their physical conditions than the condition of the church budget or the lack of progress on a building project. Those discussions may be for another time. Unless specific questions are asked (and if they are, be brief and be positive in giving answers), focus on the patient's immediate physical condition.

Use Scripture Reading and Prayer in the Healing Process

The purpose of your visit isn't to conduct a pep rally for the regional or professional sports team (although that may be a conversation starter). You're not there to do weather forecasts. You are there as an ambassador of the kingdom of God. Letting Him talk to your patient through His Word, and talking to Him on behalf of the patient is your primary mission. Also, I always instruct caregivers to take the person by the hand when a prayer is offered. Remember, when we touch, we touch for Christ.

Don't Offer a Diagnosis or a Prognosis

Face it, unless you've been to medical school, you aren't in any position to make a medical judgment call. Your opinion about patient treatments may or may not be relevant, but they should be kept to yourself.

Avoid answering patients' questions about their illness or their treatment. There are usually two sides to the medical story. You won't want to jeopardize patient treatment by expressing your opinion.

Be Courteous with Health Care Staff

You don't make hospital visits on your own. Your entire church comes with you. A friendly attitude toward hospital staff will be helpful in projecting a positive image of your local ministry.

Include the Patient's Roommate in the Visit

In a semiprivate room situation, attention should be paid to your patient's roommate. Inquiring about them or including them in your prayers (with their permission) just might result in their attendance at your church.

Be Brief

There is a reason the patient is hospitalized. They are usually in discomfort. Long conversations with the visiting pastor won't necessarily help them. Unless they seem to want a longer stay—which seldom happens—it would be best to limit your visits to a span of ten to fifteen minutes. That you are there is more important than how long you are there. Make your introduction, get to the point, and then get to the car.

I believe in holistic medicine, and I am convinced that we are a vital part of the medical team. After all, we represent the Great Physician.

36

REVIVING A
LUKEWARM CHURCH

At the dawning of the twentieth century, General William Booth of the Salvation Army prophesied that the church would experience the following points of departure if revival did not occur: Christianity without Christ, forgiveness without repentance, salvation without regeneration, religion without the Holy Spirit, politics without God, and heaven without hell.

Some years ago a pastor reviewed Booth's words and cried out to God for revival. Finally, in desperation he asked a dear saint in his church, "What will bring revival to our church?" Without hesitation she responded, "Second Chronicles seven fourteen!" The pastor was familiar with the verse but decided to do a study of it for a sermon on revival. One month later the pastor spoke from 2 Chronicles 7:14 and shared a formula for revival. The formula is as relevant today as it was then. Why? Because the symptoms are the same! Sadly, Booth's prophecy is being fulfilled.

Today's ministers are in the midst of the society that the Salvation Army founder described. Pastors will make many appeals, but none will be as important as calling a congregation to spiritual renewal—to personal revival. This is the time for the church to get serious about drawing closer to God. Too many things have come between God and His people. Fear. Worldliness. Materialism. Excess. Spiritual renewal is the greatest need. But revival in the land begins with revival in the church, and revival in the church begins with revival in the home. Subsequently, revival in the home begins with revival in the heart.

Methods

Methods are constantly evolving. What seemed to work in the past may or may not work now. Ten- to fifteen-day "revival services" will not likely find a place on the calendars of today's hurried and harried families. Almost every night of the week is filled with activity—from classes to team practices and from work schedules to community service. The twenty-first-century family doesn't have much free time.

There is still a place for an extended emphasis on spiritual renewal, however. Evangelism is still in the list of spiritual gifts, and gifted evangelists can enrich the lives of your congregation. Granted, they may preach on the same topics you've just spoken to, but a fresh voice can say the same thing with surprisingly even greater results.

A twenty-first-century call to revival will utilize a variety of methods: a revival Sunday or weekend emphasis with an evangelist, a month-long series of revival sermons by the pastor, small group studies focused on renewal, a group outing to hear a speaker or author whose specialty is spiritual renewal, retreats, assisting a church plant with a revival emphasis (the assistance itself can become a source of renewal for those involved), or a church-wide study of a book of the Bible or a book that emphasizes spiritual renewal.

Message

I was the pastor who made a study of 2 Chronicles 7:14, and then outlined it and preached from the passage—with heartwarming results.

God came, and the church experienced revival unlike anything it had ever known. My church grew at a fantastic rate all year long! The message of revival is found in my message outline.

Pray without Ceasing. The great revivals of history began with a prayer meeting. One or more souls hungry for a fresh anointing sought the Lord in times of prayer—and refused to give up until the prayer was answered. Prayer is always at the foundation of fresh anointing.

Jesus taught it. "If you then, though you are evil, know how to give good gifts to your children, how much more will your Father in heaven give the Holy Spirit to those who ask him!" (Luke 11:13).

The disciples exemplified it. Acts 4:31 reads, "After they prayed, the place where they were meeting was shaken. And they were all filled with the Holy Spirit and spoke the word of God boldly."

Practice Holiness in Living. God's chief requirement for the church doesn't have anything to do with facilities, staffing, or attendance averages. Peter wrote about it: "But just as he who called you is holy, so be holy in all you do; for it is written: 'Be holy, because I am holy'" (1 Pet. 1:15–16). Society needs to see God's holiness personified in God's people, in people who will walk the walk.

Of course, the pastor must take the lead. A heart *open to be broken* is fertile soil for God's power and presence.

Love Others. Revival flows where barriers are broken down. A people who will take the initiative to love others in spite of it all will not only be spiritually impacted; they will impact others. (See 1 John 4:20.)

Be Diligent in Outreach. When spiritual renewal comes, it won't be a secret. Everyone will know about it! And when revival comes to a people, they won't *want* to keep it a secret. A church that reaches out stands less of a chance for inner turmoil. Focusing on the needs of others takes the church's mind off its wants.

Demonstrate Generosity in Giving. Spiritual renewal always reaches the checkbook. Revival brings new vision. And visionary actions take visionary funding. Pastors who will call their people to revival are those who usually reap benefits in increased giving to their churches.

Experience the Power of the Holy Spirit. Church growth comes after soul growth. Souls filled with God's Spirit are given the spiritual edge for vibrant ministry. Every church I know of, including my own, needs God's power. And every pastor I know of—including me, as well—needs more of God's power.

When you call your people to revival, you'll probably be the first to answer.

37

HOW TO OFFER
CORRECTION

eader's Digest has a regular column called "Word Power." Readers test their wits by defining a word. Readers also use the column to learn new words. The understanding and use of words are important in every segment of society—but particularly in the church. Pastors have lost pastoral votes over a few words. Churches have lost more than one member because of words spoken. If you haven't already, you'll soon discover the fantastic power of words.

Words can be used either as bombs or bouquets. Which would you rather receive at your doorstep? A few words can be forged together and lobbed into the life of another to cause more havoc than a two-year-old at a tea party. Conversely, words can be handed out like candy to a discouraged teammate. A timely "thank you" or "I appreciate you" can do more good than a paycheck bonus. Words have the power to motivate and heal.

But those words must be sincere. How will you know when your communication is sincere? Here are some diagnostic questions to test the sincerity of your communication.

Am I Honest without Being Petty?

Honesty is always the best policy, but there is a line once crossed that can never be un-crossed—any more than a bell can be unrung. As a shepherd, you are responsible to watch sheep. Watching sheep is both a passive and an active assignment. Sheep don't always do what's right. Sheep don't always go where they should go. Sheep don't always show the right attitude toward other sheep. The shepherd has to make judgment calls on the sheep's behavior in order to guide and protect them.

Pastors shepherd people. And people don't always do what's right, go where they should go, or show the right attitude. The Apostle Paul instructed Timothy in shepherding: "Preach the Word; be prepared in season and out of season; correct, rebuke and encourage—with great patience and careful instruction" (2 Tim. 4:2).

Granted, preaching is a whole lot easier than correcting or rebuking. But correcting and rebuking are part of the pastoral ministry. There will be times when words will be formed into sentences and sentences into honest evaluations. It's never easy, but often it is necessary.

There are times when honesty may hurt those on both sides of the evaluation. Thankfully, the Holy Spirit promises to guide our speech: "We speak, not in words taught us by human wisdom but in words taught by the Spirit, expressing spiritual truths in spiritual words" (1 Cor. 2:13).

When does honesty become petty? It crosses the line when it becomes a stick rather than a staff.

Will My Words Bring Hope or Merely Hurt?

Ministers are messengers of hope. The Bible is a book of happy endings. "But now he has reconciled you by Christ's physical body through death to present you holy in his sight, without blemish and free from accusation—if you continue in your faith, established and firm, not moved from the hope held out in the gospel" (Col. 1:22–23).

Bomb or bouquet? It will depend on the words you use. The power of a well-timed word can be like a line thrown to the drowning. The line is in your hand. Ultimately it must result in saving rather than destroying.

Will Both the Giver and Receiver Benefit from This Message?

By the time Barnabas was through with him, Saul was ready to preach rather than persecute. Others had spoken harshly of the future New Testament giant. Barnabas spoke gently, using the principle of Proverbs 25:11: "A word aptly spoken is like apples of gold in settings of silver." The apples Barnabas offered were the words that strengthened Saul in faith and eventually in service.

Every conversation you have with a team member or parishioner can leave him or her in better spiritual or emotional shape than before. Give an apple; give some hope.

Do These Words Reflect the Attitude of Jesus Christ?

"Let the beauty of Jesus be seen in me," the song says. You could change the lyrics slightly: "Let the beauty of Jesus be heard through me." Most of your congregation hasn't heard an encouraging word in days or weeks. You be the first to give them one. You be the giver of life-giving words, love-giving words. A prayerful heart speaks careful words.

The ultimate test of sincerity is the ability to keep your word. People are motivated by leaders who say what they mean and mean what they say. Once a promise is given it must be kept—others will always be watching for that result.

Granted, that's not always possible. Circumstances sometimes seal off the promised actions like orange cones on a construction project; there are times when you cannot deliver on a promise that was made with good intentions. But those exceptions should be rare. In order to succeed as a spiritual leader, you must deliver on the power of a promise.

Just as words used well can empower you, so shady communication and see-through promises can sap your momentum. Brusque replies, exaggerated claims, and half-hearted assurances will eventually undermine your credibility. Wise leaders are thoughtful and deliberate in their use of words because they understand the power words have either to hurt or heal.

Honest communication, thoughtful words, and promises kept are the hallmarks of a great leader. Use words well, and they will empower your leadership for lasting results.

38

WHAT TO DO WHEN
MEMBERS LEAVE

L et's be realistic. Not everyone in your church is going to appreciate your sermons, your worship, your organizational skills, or your children! People will come to your church, and people will go from your church. Some will become members, and through circumstances often beyond your control, some will be "dis-membered." One of the trends of contemporary Christianity is the revolving door of church membership. With the advent of the megachurch age, a "pick and choose" mentality has become common.

Today's churches are often like big-box discount stores. If the price, product, or service doesn't meet the expectations of the customers, they will go to the next store. There is a place for every size church. Each has a unique quality of ministry that will appeal to some—but not to all. As one who has stood at the "revolving door" to greet those coming and going, I have learned some lessons about what to do if a member leaves.

Don't Panic

If one or more of your members packs up and leaves, don't look for the ceiling to fall. They won't be the first to leave a church, and they won't be the last. The history of the Christian church is one of banding and disbanding. Why, even the apostles had disagreements that led to division. (Remember Paul, Barnabas, and John Mark?)

A membership may come to an end, but your ministry doesn't have to. You will go on. Your church will go on; and the lessons learned can actually result in growth. In case you haven't noticed, church members and attendees are human. And humans are often emotion driven. Bruised feelings often result in soreheads. And soreheads often fight and flee over issues rather than stay and solve them.

Don't Take It Personally

The first reaction of a pastor when a member leaves is often to take all the blame. Maybe you did contribute to the boat's leaving the dock, but that doesn't mean you are a washout. You are God-called. Your appointment was sealed through prayer and authorized by the Holy Spirit. For now, you are where God wants you.

In case you've forgotten, Jesus was the greatest preacher who ever walked the face of the earth, but even He lost members of His congregation. Why, one of His trusted board members got so disenchanted, he sold the Galilean for thirty coins!

"Different strokes for different folks" isn't exactly a biblical concept, but in your heart you know it's true. You simply cannot provide everything everyone wants. If you're doing the best you can do, that's all you can do.

Talk to God about It

You are serving in God's church. You are ministering to God's people (usually!). You are using God's gifts. It stands to reason that He knows more about the situation than you do. He sees behind the hurts, the criticisms, and the misunderstandings. He knows the real reasons why people leave one church and go to another; talk to Him about it.

Get alone with God, and let His Holy Spirit speak words of wisdom to your heart and mind. Let Him affirm you through His Word. Be still and let Him do the talking. You will discover an inner healing that you never thought possible.

Learn from Your Loss

Remember, a leader is always a learner. Learn from this situation. There may be some valid reasons why a member leaves—reasons that may form the building blocks of an even more effective ministry.

Some may leave because of a weak spot in the church's overall ministry. Sometimes that simply can't be helped. For example, if you don't have the personnel, program, or children to maintain the children's ministry, you'll just have to ride it out until the children or children's workers come along. On the other hand, that weakness may result in a leader's class, where workers are recruited and trained to recruit and train additional workers. Your children's ministry may be only a leadership class away from being a viable ministry.

Keep the Communication Lines Open

Often, people leave a church because of a conflict. But sometimes they don't. Sometimes they leave because of its location or its lack of a needed program. Keep the communication lines open. Keep the former members on the mailing list, the prayer list, or the birthday and anniversary list. Congratulate their family members on accomplishments that are posted in the media. Talk about their qualities—the word will get back to them.

Don't write them off. Your church may be the place where they were saved or baptized. Or they may hold other fond remembrances of the people and the building. Consequently, your church may be the one they call on in times of crisis.

Model Christlike Behavior

Others may leave because of broken fellowship. They may be critical of the pastor or other church leaders. Don't fight back. Love them as Christ would love them. Keep them on your prayer list. Look for opportunities to show them a Christlike response. Jesus loved those who didn't love Him—even to the point of dying for them. He expects His Church to reflect the qualities of holiness. Holiness is a reflection of Christ's character—which includes forgiveness and restoration. Seek restoration. (See Rom. 12:18.)

Extinguish the Fires of Criticism

James wrote, "The tongue also is a fire, a world of evil among the parts of the body. It corrupts the whole person, sets the whole course of his life on fire, and is itself set on fire by hell" (James 3:6). Do we need to look any further for the source of criticism? Satan set the fire, but you don't have to keep the embers burning. Do your best to put the fire out.

The advice still stands: "Give it your best, and let God do the rest."

39

RECRUITING
TOP VOLUNTEERS

W	hen you find them, it's like finding gold. They are the people in your church or organization who are waiting to be a blessing to others—and to bless you at the same time. They are sought by almost every care-giving organization in your community. But they are yours. God sent them to you, even though they didn't realize it at the time. They are volunteers.

Once you discover that you can't do everything by yourself, they are the ones who are waiting in the wings. It's your job to give them their cue. Let them share the stage with you, and your performance will be enhanced. Keep them in the wings, and the curtain may fall quicker than you ever imagined.

Mobilize volunteers and you double or triple your effectiveness. Inspire those volunteers to pursue excellence, reaching for God's best in every endeavor, and the ripple effect will last for all eternity. But there is much more than merely mobilizing them. They must be fed and cared for. Napoleon said that an army marches on its stomach. But the care and feeding of volunteers means more than providing refreshments on workdays. Here's what you as the leader can do to bring out the best in your volunteers.

Appreciate Them

People don't want to be recruited; they want to be loved. They want to know that they are valuable to the church or organization. They want to know that their efforts are making a difference for Christ and the Kingdom. How do you let them know that they are appreciated?

Always Place the People Ahead of the Tasks. That's what Jesus did. Volunteers are giving valuable time to you. Acknowledge that. Like every human being, they want to be appreciated for who they are as well as for what they do.

Let Them Know They Are Needed. The landscaping around the building would look pitiful without their efforts. Families wouldn't choose the church without their help in the nursery. Sidewalks would be dangerous without their snow shoveling. Volunteers need to know that the ministry would suffer without their help.

Let Them Know You Are Their Friend. Let them know that you are available to listen to their questions or complaints. You may be their only source of encouragement, and that's part of the reason they are volunteering.

Underscore That They Are Doing God's Work. They already know how little the pay will be, but let them know how great their reward will be.

When you love and affirm the people around you, they will be drawn to your leadership. They'll do their best because they know they matter to you.

Challenge Them

Nobody wants to take on a task that seems boring—or worse, meaningless. Offer an inspiring challenge and the results will be different. When you show people that something is worthwhile, it will never seem too difficult. When they see the importance of what they're doing, they'll rise to the challenge. Always connect the dots for them: Show them how what they are doing counts for eternity.

Volunteers must be convinced that their work isn't just about setting up tables or driving the church van. They must be convinced that they are on a soul-winning journey with you. Group prayer is an important ingredient in that convincing. When you pray with your volunteer staff, make sure you translate their work into Great Commission work. Let them know that the end result is worth the immediate effort.

Direct Them

Many volunteers become discouraged because they're left to do a job without guidance. When you enlist others in the mission, always give them direction. Outline the mission for them, the overall goal that is to be reached. Cast a vision for them by painting a word picture of what the result will look like. Define the objectives, stating clearly the critical milestones that must be met. Finally, let them know that you are available for consultation or advice.

One item is often missing in directing volunteers: the job description. Ministry seems to be of greater value when it is in hard copy. Seen on paper, the volunteer's responsibility is not only clarified to the volunteer, it also gives the pastor guidance in directing their efforts.

Pray for Them

It's one thing to talk to your volunteers about their ministry; it's another talking to God about that ministry. Let your volunteers know that they are on your prayer list. God's power can work through them in miraculous ways. That quiet person who lacks self-confidence can turn into a spiritual dynamo. But God provides the dynamic. Why not take time during your sermon preparation to pray for your volunteer team's effort? And why not let your team know you prayed for them during your sermon preparation? In their mind, the importance of their work will be realized on another level!

Protect Them

Pastor, the spiritual welfare of your volunteers is in your hands. Keep them out of harm's way. Guard their family relationships by giving them some time off. Do your part to keep them true to their spouse by not putting them in vulnerable situations. Avoid teaming volunteers with members of the opposite sex. Make sure their work is a public work. After hours labors have sometimes turned to improper relationships. Your scheduling and staffing can help to protect your volunteers from tempting circumstances.

Reward Them

Nothing motivates people quite like applause. As a leader, it's up to you to start the ovation. When people achieve, call attention to it. Let them know that you've noticed, and let others know it too. Write cards of encouragement and thanks. Send affirming e-mail messages to your achievers. Be quick to offer a word of praise and a pat on the back. Reward results. You'll get more of them.

Your volunteers are like gold. Polish and protect them, and their success will not be a one-time performance.

PART 4

LEADERSHIP

Catch on fire with enthusiasm, and people will

come for miles to watch you burn.

—CHARLES WESLEY

If anyone sets his heart on being an overseer,

he desires a noble task.

—1 TIMOTHY 3:1

40

THE PREREQUISITE
FOR CHURCH LEADERSHIP

A history professor commented on Christopher Columbus's discovery of America saying that there were three significant aspects of the trip. One, before he departed, he didn't have a clue as to where he was going. Two, when he arrived, he had no idea where he was. And three, when he got ready to leave, he had no idea how to get back home.

From the back of the room a history major spoke up: "And four, he didn't have a clue as to how he was going to pay back that loan from the government!"

Thankfully, when it comes to leadership, we can be more informed. We have the greatest leadership model in the history of the world: Jesus Christ. The divine *logos* is our "final word" on the subject.

The New Testament is a survival manual for people in the trenches of leadership. One of the most influential leaders in the New Testament was John the Baptist. Crowds of people pushed and shoved to hear the words of this straight-talking messenger of the Messiah, who wore designer clothes made of camel hair.

But what was the root of John's influence?

According to John 1:23, when the religious leaders asked for John's credentials, he replied in the words of Isaiah the prophet: "I am the voice of one calling in the desert, 'Make straight the way for the Lord.'"

The Baptist knew who he was. His leadership strengths didn't come from books or seminars, conferences or conventions. As vital as those edge-sharpening tools may be, John's authority came from the power that flowed from his connection to Jesus Christ, the Messiah. And John's message to the masses was always the same: "He must become greater; I must become less" (John 3:30).

What would John the Baptist tell us if he were conducting a seminar on Christian leadership?

Connection to Christ

Your power for leadership is in your connection to Jesus Christ. John the Baptist lived Christ's message: "I am the vine; you are the branches. If a man remains in me and I in him, he will bear much fruit; apart from me you can do nothing" (John 15:5). That was the key quality of John's ministry—and it should be ours. Our power for leadership is not self-propelled; it comes from our relationship with the risen Savior.

It is a connection that is maintained by surrendering our ambitions to Him and gaining His vision and strength. "I am the true vine, and my Father is the gardener. He cuts off every branch in me that bears no fruit, while every branch that does bear fruit he prunes so that it will be even more fruitful" (15:1–2).

A Christian leader will never lead people forward for Christ without first taking his or her own trip to the Cross. Without the electricity of Calvary's flow, human leaders are powerless. There is no bypass. Personal faith in Jesus Christ and the empowerment of His Spirit is the great prerequisite for Christian leadership.

Concentrated on the Mission

Your purpose for leadership is in your understanding of Christ's mission. Jesus didn't come to earth to establish a corporate dynasty. He came to earth to provide a continuing dynamic. John 10:10 reads, "The thief comes only to steal and kill and destroy; I have come that they may have life, and have it to the full." Everything Jesus did during His three-year ministry was to enhance the lives of those around Him. Of course, His greatest provision was salvation. But He also taught His followers how to achieve their best goals. He helped them to turn their weaknesses into strengths. For example, fishermen were encouraged to take it to the next level and become fishers of men. Pastors were encouraged to become leaders. Young Christians were encouraged to become living examples.

Your purpose as a Christian leader is to model Christ's purpose in bringing out Christian excellence in fellow Christians. Those whom you lead should be better off because of their interaction with you.

Founded on God's Word

Your plans for leadership are in your understanding of God's Word. John's gospel records, "Jesus replied, 'If anyone loves me, he will obey my teaching. My Father will love him, and we will come to him and make our home with him. He who does not love me will not obey my teaching. These words you hear are not my own; they belong to the Father who sent me'" (14:23–24).

You won't have to look far to find a model for leading others. Jesus has already addressed the qualities of leadership.

First, He concentrated on sharing leadership plans with a select few. His disciples became students of His leadership, and He gladly taught them the ropes.

Second, He expanded His influence through the lives of others. He not only taught the twelve, He commissioned them to ministry.

Third, He recognized the importance of rest and restoration. He knew that the daily grinds of leadership would demand a retreat from them.

Fourth, He established an action plan for meeting objectives. People were delegated in teams. Goals were announced—ministry in Jerusalem, Judea, and Samaria. Supplies were provided—His Word, His presence, His power. Affirmation was given—they were promised an even greater influence than His own. And victories were celebrated— they were told that angels would rejoice over their accomplishments.

Godly leadership always takes the high road. There are no shortcuts in effective ministry. But the arrival is worth every mile of the journey.

41

FIVE MARKS
OF A GREAT LEADER

Great leaders know that their achievement does not depend on someone else's failure. There is more than enough success to go around. The most effective leaders are not afraid to help others reach their goals; they believe in the power of the win-win situation.

Author and motivational speaker Zig Ziglar says you can get everything you want if you help enough others get what they want. To do that, you'll have to have an attitude of openness. That may require a change of mind.

Rather than looking out only for their own interests, great leaders learn to ask win-win questions like these: What can I do for you? What can we do together? How can this benefit both of us? Learn to ask, "How can I help others succeed?" and you will succeed as well.

A leader who is always looking for credit will soon be a solo performer. No team will follow a truly selfish leader. The team may establish a good work regimen and perform well, but unless the members respect their leader, it will not excel.

The best leaders display that seldom-seen virtue called humility. They discover real worth in terms of their ability to generate team excellence, not personal recognition. There are five marks of greatness of a leader.

Great Leaders Don't Care Who Gets the Credit as Long as the Job Gets Done

Actions take precedence over accolades. Goals are more important than gold. Ribbons are incidental to right behavior. Great leaders don't draw attention to themselves; they express appreciation for the contributions of others. Great leaders take a bow for the team. They give credit where credit is due—to the team that brought about the success.

All of us know what it's like to see someone take the credit for what was achieved by our own sweat and tears. The feeling is an emptiness that may never again be filled—we may sigh a "What's the use" when another assignment is given to us.

Great Leaders Are Willing to Put the Mission Ahead of Their Personal Agenda

Great leaders have discovered the greater joy of giving their lives for something worthwhile. The purpose, mission, and objectives of the organization are paramount, while the personality and personal achievements of the leader are secondary. They know that what they have done as individuals is far less important than what they can accomplish with and through others.

Of course that characteristic is linked to the leader's knowledge of the purpose, mission, and objectives of the organization. When the leader fully knows where he or she is heading, it will be easier to give direction to others. And lighting the path for others is of far more importance than basking in a spotlight.

Great Leaders Are Quick to Forgive

Little people hold grudges; big people forgive and forget. Little people nurse insults and look for revenge; big people let bygones be bygones. All great leaders are big people. They earn respect but never demand it. They avoid petty squabbles and develop thick skins.

Jesus modeled the greatest leadership. Whether addressing the city that rejected Him, the woman caught in adultery, or the thief on the cross who finally acknowledged Him, the heart of the Great Leader was a heart of compassion and mercy. Can the Christian leader do any less than follow the example of Christ? Of course not!

Great Leaders Are Energized by the Achievements of Others

All good leaders realize that they themselves can never accomplish all they dream of; others must carry out their vision. So they invest in others, encourage them, train them, and enable them to succeed. The best leaders realize that there's plenty of successes to go around, so they help those around them reach for the stars.

Great leaders bask in the glow of team members who have reached their predetermined goals. They are quick to hand out ribbons of encouragement and congratulations.

Great Leaders Freely Give to Those Who Deserve It Most

They know that they are highly skilled, yet they realize that their success depends on the contribution of others. They know that there are no "little people" in the organization; every person's contribution is significant. Good leaders know how to say "Well done," and they say it often. They don't assume that a team member knows their work is appreciated. They make sure it is acknowledged—either verbally or in print.

Everyone tends to make forward motion when they are given a pat on the back. Appreciation is one of the great motivators—often more than promotions or pay raises.

Enjoying great success does not depend on having a great ego. In fact, the opposite is almost always true. Those who think the most of themselves are usually respected little by others. But those who show respect to others in lieu of personal recognition are given the greater respect—respect that is earned and not demanded.

Leader, what is your "credit" rating?

Do you want to advance your own goals? Learn to put others first.

42

CASTING FAITH-INSPIRED VISION

I f you can't see the future, you'll never get there. Vision planning is an essential skill for every leader. But there's something even more important. There is a leadership trait even more vital than seeing the future—and that is believing it. Leaders who lack faith lack the force to make their vision a reality. Faith is an essential ingredient for successful leadership in any organization.

The Bible says, "And without faith it is impossible to please God, because anyone who comes to him must believe that he exists and that he rewards those who earnestly seek him" (Heb. 11:6). As Christian leaders, we believe both in God and in the power of His promises. We know that He is there and that He will do for us what He has said He will do. We lead by faith.

I've always admired the person who is willing to be the first swimmer in a group to dive into the water. It may be 60 degrees Fahrenheit—with the water temperature several degrees cooler—but there is always someone in the crowd who is willing to take the first plunge.

The best part is the swimmer's bold claim, usually delivered through chattering teeth: "Come on in . . . the water's f-f-fine!" Faith is willing to be the first to take the plunge. People of faith are always early adopters of God's plan. One of the best examples of faith is Noah, that intrepid sailor who was willing to build a boat when there wasn't a drop of water in sight. His story provides a lesson in faith for every leader.

Faith Believes without Proof

Noah built the ark without ever seeing rain. That's true for most of the things we do that require faith—we have to believe beyond what we can see for ourselves. We begin with our most basic article of faith—belief in God. We don't need to see Him to know that He is real. Peter reminds us, "Though you have not seen him, you love him; and even though you do not see him now, you believe in him and are filled with an inexpressible and glorious joy" (1 Pet. 1:8).

Faith is *believing without proof*, whether it's faith in God's promises to us, faith in His eternal plan for the world, or faith in His particular plan for our lives. We trust God, even though we can't see all the details. We put our hand in the unseen hand and march on—even in the face of adversity.

Faith Stands Alone

A second lesson from Noah's journey is that faith stands alone. He and his family were the only God-fearing believers in his community—actually, in the world! Yet that man of God would not be intimidated. He stuck to the plan even when he had to go it alone. People of faith don't need to be members of an elite club; they're willing to cling to the promises of God even when that means being different from others. To stand against the crowd and for Jesus requires a firm conviction of the truth of God's Word. And Noah's experiences drive home another point worth pondering: The crowd is often wrong.

The classic expression "It's lonely at the top" is true for every Christian leader. There are times when he or she will have to go it alone. Will have to fight the tides of tradition. Will have to endure the vote of the crowd in the "Most likely to succeed" category. Often the leader and follower part ways over principles—principles important enough to live or die for. Yet the leader is willing to march bravely into the arena, is willing to take a stand even if it means losing popularity contests.

Faith Takes Action

James wrote, "Faith by itself, if it is not accompanied by action, is dead" (James 2:17). He might have been writing about Noah. That man of God not only believed that it would rain but also did something about it—he built a boat. He was willing to construct a monument to his faith in God's Word. He was willing to follow God's action plan. He was willing to live by the owner's manual—even if it meant a cruise without reservations in the luxury cabin.

What is the action to which God is calling you? Will you step out in faith and just do it?

Faith Sees Results

Being a person of faith means being willing to trust God regardless of the outcome. Noah was. Yet the promises of God are true, and those who rely on them are never disappointed. God promised Noah that it would rain—and did it ever! Having acted in faith, Noah and his family were saved from the flood. They believed that it would happen, and they saw it come to pass.

When you step out and follow God, you will see results too. I promise you it won't be as dramatic as Noah's flood—God has promised that there will be no repeat performance of that event. But when you stake your faith on God's promises and act accordingly, the results will be no less meaningful in your life and ministry. Believe it, and you will see it.

So, when you pray for rain, wear a raincoat!

43

BUILDING A
WINNING TEAM

Team building is a vital skill for any pastor. Gone are the days when the pastor could be an autocratic leader. Church boards and church members who are used to having their say in the workplace demand to be included in decision making. Building a solid team is essential.

And it's smart. You'll accomplish more in ministry if you learn to tap the resources of others. Team members are not a threat to your leadership; they're essential to your success! It's been said that individuals sign autographs, endorse products, and grant interviews, but teams win championships. You will do more, gain more goodwill, and live with less stress if you have a strong team around you.

What's the strength of your team? Is it a real team or merely a collection of individuals? Is your team focused? Are team members well equipped and highly motivated? You can build a winning team. Keep working, and keep working together. The Kingdom needs good teams and strong leaders. The Kingdom needs you!

The next time you see geese flying south, think about the reason they always fly in formation. Scientists figure that the V formation adds at least 71 percent to the flight range of the flock. By working together, geese can travel nearly twice as far as any one of them could alone.

That's teamwork!

Investing in a team pays long-term dividends. Your ultimate success in ministry is not conditioned on building capacity or programming expertise. Your success will rest on your ability and desire to invest in others to build a winning team. Here are six essential skills for developing your dream team in ministry.

Learn the Art of Delegation

Delegation is an art. Most pastors are afraid to delegate and thus find themselves on a ministry treadmill, hoping they don't get "voted off the island." Delegation involves setting expectations, providing direction, allowing for creativity, negotiating deadlines, checking on results, and rewarding performance. Don't be threatened by the availability or the ability of others. Enlist them to build your team.

Affirm Others

Question: Who are the most important people in your ministry? Typically, they are the people you clap for. Most often, we applaud those who perform some public ministry like leadership, music, or teaching. How about giving a standing ovation to the prayer warriors in your church or to those who invite unsaved friends to attend? Every team needs people with a variety of skills. If you honor only the shot makers and never the shot takers, your team will lose momentum. Whom you applaud, you empower.

Cheer for your team.

Provide Adequate Support

When people are trained and commissioned for a task but are not given adequate support, they usually complete their assignment. The problem? They won't volunteer again. But when a person is trained, motivated, and given the resources to succeed, he or she will feel a part of the team. When you delegate, ask, "Do you have everything you need?" For your organization, the answer will mean the difference between forward motion and standing still.

If the answer is positive, you've gained a long-term contributor. But if the answer is in the negative it's time for regrouping. Has the training been adequate? Is the job description clear? Are volunteer helpers available? Does the team member have appropriate skills? Is there a better place to use the team member's abilities?

Motivate Teammates

People are motivated by many things: money, guilt, and recognition to name a few. But the best motivator is the eternal one. Always direct your team's attention to the eternal value of what they are doing. They're not just setting up chairs; they're serving Christ's Church. They're not merely teaching Sunday school, they're shaping lives. What they do lasts forever. Remind your teammates of that.

Also let them know that God keeps the books. In the words of a great preacher, there will be a "payday someday."

Evaluate Results

If you don't care whether your team wins, then there's no need to keep score. But if you're interested in success, you'll need to evaluate the team's performance. It will help you to improve. Did we reach our goal? What could have been done better? How will we avoid making the same mistake next time? What can I do to improve results? Ask these questions regularly, and you'll build a winning team.

Team evaluation times should be a time of positive reinforcement, not a time of embarrassment. The leader's attitude and the atmosphere of the evaluation make the evaluation process helpful, not hurtful.

Reward Performance

When your team has a victory, celebrate! Point out the contribution of each member. Let all of them know how important they are to the whole. Never let a milestone go by unnoticed. Find a reason to cheer. Celebrating wins will energize your team for further victories.

Great teams don't just happen. They're shaped by great leaders. Pour your energy into others, and they'll pour their energy into the mission.

44

DIRECTING ATTENTION

I have a vision," one leader announced confidently. Then he frowned. "Or is it a mission? Or a goal? Oh, who cares! God knows what I mean."

But God may be the only one who does! Those who follow will struggle to know where they're going if the leader cannot articulate the vision clearly. Everyone has more confidence in a leader who is sure of the destination and how to get there than in a leader who plays it by ear.

People just aren't prone to invest their time, talent, or treasure in an organization—and its leader—that doesn't have either a mission or a purpose. There are too many bidding for their skills or character qualities. To get quality team members, the organization and its leader must have a focus—a vision for what it wants to accomplish.

Here are the five basic concepts of vision casting. Master them and people will follow you.

Mission

Mission is the overall goal, and it never changes. This is the big-picture statement that answers the question "Why are we here?" In fact, many mission statements begin with the words "We exist in order to . . ." You could plant a church on every corner of the community, but that doesn't mean those churches will have any decided impact on that community. They first need a direction, a stated reason for being.

Your church needs a mission. It needs to understand why it occupies its particular piece of property. It needs to know why it will hire its leaders, staff its ministry, or appoint its volunteers. Otherwise, the focus of the ministry will be like pellets fired from a shotgun: powerful but scattered.

Jesus had a mission: "The Son of Man came to seek and to save what was lost" (Luke 19:10). One of the great New Testament leaders, Paul, had a mission: "I am not seeking my own good but the good of many, so that they may be saved" (1 Cor. 10:33). Notice how his mission mirrored that of the Master. Our mission must always be formed on that same foundation. The church is simply on a mission that was begun in the life of its Leader.

Your mission will include the *who* and *what* of your ministry, as well as the *where*. On whom will you focus your ministry—what demographic? It will also include the what—what organization will need to be formed in order to reach that demographic? What personnel will be needed? What will be the flow of your material resources? And most important, what part will Jesus have in your ministry?

Vision

The Bible says, "In his heart a man plans his course, but the LORD determines his steps" (Prov. 16:9). Mapping the course—casting the vision—of your church's ministry is a next important step. A vision provides focus for what the organization will become or accomplish in this particular place at this particular time. Vision should be *local, specific,* and *inspiring.* For example, your church might declare, "Our vision is to reach every home in this community with the gospel of Jesus Christ." Or your business vision might state, "We will become the largest provider of service in the county."

Your vision is your spiritual dream. It is the foundation on which you will make your ministry impact.

Values

Values are the nonnegotiable characteristics of an organization—its heart and soul. They guide leaders and enable them to say the crucial word no. If a new project is proposed, it must pass through the grid of values to determine whether it fits the organization's identity and purpose. If it will, then it is moved to the next level of planning. If it does not match the organization's values, it gets the big N-O.

The Word of God is the church's "values vault." From its treasure the plans and resources of its ministry are directed. Leader, you are always on guard duty, watching for any drifting from the values established in the Scriptures.

Strategy

Strategy is the plan for accomplishing the vision. It incorporates all relevant considerations in a way that provides the most efficient means of getting the job done. An effective strategy includes strategic objectives, intermediate and long-term plans that advance the vision.

Goals

Goals represent what the organization desires to accomplish within a certain time frame. Goals must be specific, measurable, and dated. A church's goal might be to win twenty-five people to Christ within one year. A business may aim to increase production by 5 percent in thirteen weeks. Goals become the objective criteria for measuring effectiveness and determining progress.

Know your mission. See your vision clearly. Establish your goals. Communicate them effectively, and you will likely succeed.

45

EVALUATING
OPPORTUNITIES

T he husband-and-wife vacationers had paid hundreds of dollars for their getaway to an exclusive Caribbean resort. Included in the package was a scuba-diving lesson. Clear blue waters beckoned as they donned air tanks and swim fins and then leaned backward into the water.

At thirty feet below the surface, incredible beauty was an immediate payoff for the money invested. The husband wrote a note to his wife on a waterproof chalkboard: "This is great!"

Suddenly, another person appeared in the water. Dressed in street clothes and wearing no diving equipment, this swimmer energetically swam up to the surface, then casually floated back down to the ocean floor. The vacationers watched in amazement as he repeated this cycle several times. Finally, they swam over to him and wrote on the chalkboard, "Why no gear?"

The man, his face turning purple, grabbed the chalkboard and wrote frantically, "Boat sank. I'm drowning!"

Every leader has felt that way at some time. You're surrounded by beautiful opportunities but have that sinking feeling: too much to do, too little time, not enough resources, no help.

Keeping your head above water demands that you maximize energy by making the most of your opportunities. Leaders make dozens of decisions every day. In fact, before you get that first cup of coffee, you've probably made several choices. Casual or business? Loafers or wing tips? Sweater or blazer? Old Spice or Ralph Lauren? But the most important choices you make are not about appearance—they're about importance. The things you decide to do—the things you decide are important—will directly influence your energy flow throughout the day. It's vital that you evaluate every opportunity to determine what matters most in every situation.

Here are four questions that will help you evaluate the importance of any opportunity.

Is It God-Honoring?

Will your decided action maintain its integrity once it's strained through the filter of your faith? If it's not a Kingdom priority, it has the potential to drain your energy instead of enhancing it. Elmer Towns said, "Greatness involves more than measurable achievement; it starts with the leader's heart and not his head."

There is no better advice than Jesus' admonition to seek first the kingdom of God. Focusing on the kingdom of earth may result in high attendance days, beautiful new facilities, and successful capital campaigns. But all of those without a deep commitment to the Kingdom will be worthless in eternity.

Does It Have an Eternal Dimension?

Does the proposed action merely result in gaining wealth or recognition on earth, or does it invest in eternity? Actions centered entirely in the temporal are energy drainers. Just ask someone who is caught in a credit trap. They are consumed with trying to impress people with something new. Will your proposed action increase your stock in the things of earth or will it add to your account in heaven's savings and loan?

Will It Add Quality or Merely Quantity?

Those "unclaimed jewels" of Jesus' time, Mary and Martha, struggled with this very issue (Luke 10:38–42). Mary was too "heavenly," and Martha was too "earthly." Where's the balance? That's the important question. Once you reach adulthood, chores are usually a choice. But keep adding chores, and the result is fewer choices! Chores begin to dominate and soon siphon your energy reserves.

How Will It Affect My Family?

The family is a God-given institution, and as such should be a priority. Interpersonal relationships with those we love the most should be joyous, not tumultuous. Adding another opportunity to your calendar might not necessarily be good for the family. It's like the elderly man who presented his letter and some pocket change to the postal clerk. The clerk said, "I'm sorry, sir. This letter is too heavy. You're going to have to add another stamp." The man replied sharply, "And I suppose that's going to make it lighter!?"

Every day you have a "cash" reserve of 1,440 minutes. You can't afford to waste them on any activity that doesn't add value to your life and advance the goals of your organization. Because you *can* do something is no reason that you *should*.

Evaluate every opportunity carefully. God wants you to succeed, and He will provide everything necessary for your success. But He gave the greatest opportunity: choice. He longs for you to be led by His Spirit, to carefully choose between the immediate and the important, to seek His will above your wants, and to rest in the assurance of His presence.

46

How to
Recruit Leaders

As a leader, you're only as good as the team that surrounds you. No manager ever won the World Series. No coach ever won the Super Bowl. You need strong players to get out on the field and implement the vision. A leader must have a team.

As a leader, your first imperative is to discover the God-given vision for your ministry. Your second challenge is to develop the team that will help you achieve it. As Vince Lombardi put it, "People who work together will win, whether it be against complex football defenses, or the problems of modern society." That's especially true in ministry settings—you need a strong team working together in order to achieve.

That means you can't do it alone. No matter how gifted you are, no matter how energetic, no matter how determined, you need the support of capable associates.

Good teams start with good team members. They don't usually advertise themselves in the classified section, and they're seldom written of in Christian magazines. In fact, good team members are usually hard to find.

Early in the church's history, the apostles faced the need to recruit a leader. They had to replace Judas, the one who was lost. Peter was chairman of the search committee, and the steps the committee took under his leadership offer insights into the development of an effective leadership team.

Search in the Right Direction

Author and denominational leader Earle L. Wilson told of speaking at a conference in a lakeside retreat center where one conferee had a frustrating expedition in a canoe. No matter how hard he tried, the canoeist insisted, he and his partner couldn't make any progress.

"How were you positioned in the canoe?" Wilson asked. The "sailor" gave an interesting reply. "We were facing each other," he said. They made no progress because they were pushing in opposite directions.

Peter recognized that the team needed to press on in the right direction, even after one of its key players failed. (See Acts 1:15–20.) "It is written in the book of Psalms," Peter pointed out, "'May his place be deserted; . . . May another take his place of leadership" (verse 20). "We need to push on," Peter was saying. "We need to continue fulfilling our God-given purpose."

What is the purpose of your ministry? Identify potential leaders who are "on board" with your aims.

Offer Leadership Training

Leaders don't grow on trees. They grow in classrooms. There are those who have leadership qualities and don't know it! They must learn to discover them. A regular leadership class, including spiritual gifts tests, will often see its most faithful students in a future leadership role.

The classroom setting is a good place to spot those who have leadership qualities. The class may also include leadership assignments, which will also identify leader qualities.

Take a Good Look Around You

Some of your best workers may be potential leaders. The Apostle Peter gave us a hint: "It is necessary to choose one of the men who have been with us the whole time the Lord Jesus went in and out among us. . . . For one of these must become a witness with us of his resurrection" (Acts 1:21–22). When recruiting leaders, start with your own team. The best candidate may be standing right next to you!

Who are those whom you can count on to carry out a plan? Who are the most dependable? The most devoted? The least likely to complain about their duties? The most teachable? They are prime candidates for your leadership team.

Ask the Holy Spirit to Guide You

The Holy Spirit is committed to being your guide. (See John 16:13.) The pathways of ministry are dotted with the walking wounded who have ignored the still, small voice of the Spirit and listened to the crowd. What took early church leaders forty days of prayer and fasting to decide, modern leaders often settle in forty seconds!

The focus of the apostles' search committee was prayer: "So they proposed two men: Joseph called Barsabbas (also known as Justus) and Matthias. Then they prayed . . ." (Acts 1:23–24).

Before making a final selection, the apostles submitted the matter for the Holy Spirit's approval. They prayed, He answered, and the right choice was made. Don't attempt to make a recruiting decision—or settle any important question—without seeking the guidance of the Holy Spirit.

Your team will only be as strong as the leaders on it. Recruit good leaders, and you will have a successful team. If you are faithful in the recruitment process, you will multiply your efforts and effectiveness. If you neglect to take the appropriate steps in the recruitment process, you will multiply your ineffectiveness. It's your choice.

47

TIPS FOR
TRAINING LEADERS

You can't do it alone. I can't. Nobody can. No matter how talented, creative, bright, and energetic a leader you may be (and you are!), you can't do the work of ministry by yourself. Every leader needs a team.

Are you building one?

Creating a strong team will multiply your efforts. Did you ever wish for just one more hour in a day or one more day in a week? What if you could add twenty-four hours to every day and gain an additional seven days each week? Recruiting key players for your team will increase your productivity. As others own your vision, they will help you make it a reality.

Building a strong team will add longevity to your ministry. Have you noticed that individual athletes burn out much sooner than team players? Gymnasts and figure skaters are lucky to be competitive at age eighteen. But Michael Jordan returned to professional basketball at thirty-eight! Relying on "bench strength" will keep your energy level high. We need you for the long haul; create a team that will help you stay in the game.

Every organization needs leaders. As a leader, one of your primary challenges is to identify and recruit other leaders who will staff your team. In that recruitment process you must identify leadership qualities in potential team members. These include vision that looks beyond the present, integrity that characterizes lifestyle, risk-taking when others shrink back, patience that equalizes the pressures that occur, and kindness that binds people together as a golden chain.

But recruiting leaders is just the first step. In order to be effective, every leader must be trained. In fact, these leaders, once trained, must become responsible for training others! The focus of a leadership team should be on the systematic equipping of workers. The Apostle Paul modeled this "training chain" theory in his advice to Pastor Timothy: "And the things you have heard me say in the presence of many witnesses entrust to reliable men who will also be qualified to teach others" (2 Tim. 2:2).

In order to do that, you'll need to conduct training sessions. Why?

The Need for Information

This is the information age. The age of breaking news and exclusive interviews. The reporter who breaks the story gives his or her media outlet the edge. Modern technology allows on-the-spot information. It is the information age for the church, as well. Every successful organization has a constant and consistent flow of form, fact, and philosophy that keeps the organization on course.

Every worker needs to be acquainted with the church's mission (philosophy), be advised of current data (fact), and given appropriate materials (form) in order to be effective.

The Need for Instruction

Form, facts, and philosophies are meaningless unless they can be practically applied to the lives of people. Every leader needs training on the how-to of his or her ministry. Think of the time and money that corporations spend on training executives! If secular leaders understand the value of training, how much more should the Church be willing to invest in its leaders!

Some of the most important times you will spend with your leaders will be times of training. Jesus modeled that for us. He combined ministry with training. The disciples learned to love and respect the Master as He poured His life into them. One-to-one or in small groups, the disciples learned the spiritual ropes.

The Need for Involvement

Training sessions allow for a time of sharing purpose and ideas. What may not be learned in a formal classroom may be learned in an informal discussion time. For example, the veteran leader may have just the right technique for recruiting staff that a rookie leader will pick up during discussion.

Mutual trust forms the foundation for team building. Any opportunity you may give your leadership team for shared training gives them the advantage of personal support and shared wisdom.

The Need for Inspiration

The athletic team huddle is not only a time when plays are called, but also a time when encouragement is given. There is an excitement that results from getting together during the game for a time of reflection, instruction, and motivation. Training sessions offer that same kind of inspiration.

Of course, the coach is sending in the plays. He or she is fully involved in the game plan. Your personal leadership—from the sidelines or on the field as a player-coach will affirm the team players and inspire them to exceed their personal best.

Recruit leaders with the attitude and vision to accomplish something great. And give them the training they'll need to achieve it! A changed congregation begins with leaders who have been given fresh ideas and renewed direction.

48

SEVEN TEAMS YOU NEED

Jesus didn't choose only one apostle. He appointed twelve. That should be our first clue that teamwork is an important part of biblical leadership. It won't be our last.

Paul and Barnabas functioned as a team to choose the elders of the local churches they planted. Paul teamed up with Timothy when sending a letter to the church at Philippi, which included elders, deacons, and congregation members. Elders functioned as a team when they were challenged by Peter to shepherd the people of God. (See 1 Peter 5:1–5.) Deacons functioned as a team in caring for the Hellenistic widows in Acts 6. Teamwork is often seen in the Bible, and it remains a vital part of effective leadership.

How are your team building skills? What level of teamwork do you display with your peers and superiors? Are you a team builder? Are you a team player? You will accomplish much more if you are, and you will ultimately be more effective for the Kingdom.

The value of teamwork is exemplified in sports. For example, college coaches must deal with constant turnovers among their players, and that's true for most leaders as well. An organization is not one team but many. Within every successful enterprise, teams are constantly forming, performing, and disbanding as the needs and objectives of the group change. To be successful, you must learn to identify the various teams that are needed within your organization, and form them effectively.

There are seven types of teams you will need at various points in your leadership.

Problem-Solving Teams

A problem-solving team is designed to complete a particular task or solve a problem, then disband. Committees naturally become stagnant when they don't have a clear objective. This team must always be focused on a particular goal and maintain a sense of urgency about reaching the objective. A problem-solving team can respond faster than a standing committee, and its members can be selected based on the demands of the task.

Specialty Teams

Some assignments require the expertise of people who are competent in a certain field. A specialty team typically goes beyond the work of the problem-solving team, assembling experts to deal with challenges at a higher level. Specialty teams may deal with issues that take a year or longer to resolve. These teams usually demand a higher level of commitment from members.

Leadership Teams

The senior leaders and governing board of an organization comprise its leadership team. (If you don't have a leader, you don't have a team.) A leadership team needs someone at the helm. This team functions as the nerve center of the organization, issuing assignments and gathering feedback from others. All organizations have a leadership team because all organizations have leaders. However, not all leadership teams function as a team. When there is conflict in an organization, it can often be traced to the leadership team. Getting the leaders of any group to work together is a primary responsibility of the leader.

Mentoring Teams

The title sounds formal, but the team assignment is not. Often, mentoring teams meet informally to discuss one facet of the group's work. For example, workers in parallel positions may meet once a week for coffee and to discuss common issues, problems, and ideas. While there is no formal agenda, the group functions as a learning lab for the members. Good leaders encourage, and sometimes initiate, mentoring teams.

Ad Hoc Teams

Ad hoc teams are similar to problem-solving teams, but they usually have less authority. Their purpose is to investigate, gather information, and present options to a decision-making body. An ad hoc team, for example, might be assembled to review the pay patterns for the company. The team would include representatives from all levels of the organization and would present recommendations for action to the organization's leaders.

High-Performance Teams

High-performance teams are specialized and spontaneous. These teams usually have an ongoing responsibility that calls for creativity and the application of skill. A church in Washington has a high-performance worship team. It meets informally to design upcoming worship services. Members have a high level of skill and commitment to the task. High-performance teams are often self-managed.

Cross-Training Teams

Cross-training teams cover areas where weaknesses have been discovered. These teams are empowered to make decisions on the fly, where a delay in the process would prevent reaching important goals. Cross-training teams are usually interdisciplinary and include decision makers from each area represented.

Getting players to work together is much easier if each one knows his or her role and responsibility. If you carefully define the nature and mission of a team, it will function more effectively. Master the art of team creation, and you will master the art of teamwork.

49

ENSURING INSTITUTIONAL INTEGRITY

W e've heard it too many times.

The church is thriving and growing, finances are solid, and momentum strong. There's just one problem—the pastor is forced to resign because of a character issue. Suddenly, the organization is in chaos.

The corporation is booming. Sales are up, the workforce is motivated, and the stock value is rising. There's just one problem—the CEO has cooked the books. Within weeks, hundreds of people are unemployed.

It is never enough to be efficient, capable, or talented. A leader must have character, first and foremost. We must maintain our integrity if we are to lead successfully.

You and I have an obligation to meet, a sacred trust to uphold. We must guard our hearts, actions, and reputations. There's a lot riding on any leader—especially a pastor. We must be people of integrity.

As captain of your church's ship, you are responsible for charting the course, recruiting the sailors, keeping the sails up, watching out for the rocks, and being ready to man the lifeboats. You carry a heavy responsibility—the integrity of your "vessel" is at stake!

Integrity is a direct reflection of you. Great caution should be taken to make sure your organization stands tall in the Kingdom and in the community. Here are some tips for leading with integrity.

Stay on Course

More than likely, you have taken time to construct a statement of purpose—documenting the "whats," the "whys," and the "wherefores" of your organization. Your next important task will be to keep your organization focused on that purpose.

Paul encouraged all New Testament leaders to stay on the same page by ". . . being like-minded, having the same love, being one in spirit and purpose" (Phil. 2:2). Make sure the activities, schedules, and objectives of your organization complement your reason for being.

Don't Overpromise

The integrity of many churches has been tarnished by one-hundred-dollar ads for ten-dollar programs. If it's not going to be the best, biggest, most spectacular, and most heavenly event on the face of the earth, don't promise that it will. You know the disappointment of ordering a fast food sandwich from the look of the picture over the counter. Pictures and words are often deceiving. That shouldn't be the case for the church program.

Be Open about Plans and Programs

A lack of openness about organizational programs or plans is a surefire integrity killer. One senior pastor invited a youth pastor to join the staff of his congregation. Unfortunately, the senior pastor neglected to mention it to the church's board members. Imagine the embarrassment of that prospective staff member when he arrived on the scene. Not only was the position withdrawn, but the senior pastor lost his parking space within a couple of months.

In this case, the pastor's integrity should have begun in the boardroom. Intentionally—or unintentionally—deceiving the leaders of the congregation made it difficult for succeeding pastors. A lack of integrity has a wide influence.

Open the Books

People want to be informed when the cash both flows and ebbs. One of the most important documents an organization can publish is its financial statement. Your congregation likely has read the newspapers and listened to or watched the news before they arrived for worship. Too many financial fiascos in the corporate world are fresh on their minds.

Discretionary funds will be available to those organizations that show discretion in the handling of their finances.

Promote Purity

The leader must create a wholesome ministry environment. Schedule ministry in groups rather than two-by-two. Encourage—even demand—that volunteers take regular time off from ministry. Guard interaction times to avoid "borderline" jokes and conversations. Church leaders must not contribute to the delinquency of a congregational member by not guarding the ministry environment.

Focus on the Main Thing

Ministry-focused organizations have as their purpose the mandate to win souls and build up believers. Other activities are viable only if they eventually lead back to the main track—evangelism. Your mission and purpose is the cornerstone of your every church activity. You must answer to the Christ of the Church. What He stands for is more important than anything else. And you must stand with Him.

War hero and former president Dwight D. Eisenhower said, "If a man's associates find him guilty of phoniness, if they find that he lacks forthright integrity, he will fail." The first great need for every leader is integrity. Maintain yours, and your church will too.

50

FIVE WAYS TO EXPAND YOUR EXPERTISE

The story is told of a farmer who posted this sign on the pasture fence: "Trespassers welcome. Just be sure to cross the field in 9.9 seconds. The bull can make it in 10!" In this fast-moving information age, it's easy to get left behind. Leaders stay ahead of those charging bulls by staying alert and keeping themselves informed.

Good leaders don't try to be experts in every area. They know what they know and what they don't know. They understand the limitations of their wisdom and experience, and they fill in the gaps by asking questions, seeking counsel, and learning from others.

People who don't ask for counsel make unnecessary mistakes. Great leaders are not bashful about asking for advice and not skittish about taking it. They cultivate counselors. They work on developing a network of associates who can plug modules of skill and experience into their lives. Here are a few of the places outstanding leaders look for advice.

At Home

The best leaders are sensitive to the abilities and experience of their own associates. They seek input from the team and ask questions. They know there is no shame in being ignorant, but it's a crime to be negligent. They freely ask for information from those they know best.

Some of your best advice may come from a staff meeting. You've appointed people because of their abilities. You've added staff because of their natural wisdom. Why not utilize those skills? Great leaders are not afraid to humble themselves in the face of an overwhelming problem. They're not afraid to bring the problem to the table and ask the questions that will prompt answers from those around them.

In Print

Leaders are readers. They learn how to pick the meat off an article or news item and leave the bones. They know what's in the news, and they keep up on trade journals. There is always a book on their nightstand.

They either subscribe to or borrow magazines that relate to their ministry field. They transfer management advice from a magazine to their research folders.

Online

Leaders are surfers. But they're smart enough to stay out of dangerous waters! They know that an answer to a project may be just an Internet search away—and they're careful not to be sidetracked to the wrong side of the tracks! They know how to use the unfathomable resources of the Web for tips and clues to ministry success. But they choose the trusted Web sites, and they favor those that offer Christian counsel.

At Workshops

Continuing education opportunities abound in nearly every field, and the best leaders attend them, keeping current on their business or profession. They know that the price of registration for a good learning opportunity will be more than made up by increased sales, improved efficiency, or an influx of good ideas. They go to learn, and they take others with them.

Not every workshop will ring the bell of wisdom. But it is said that if you can bring one good idea home from a workshop or seminar—usually from the predominant theme—it will be worth every dollar or hour invested.

Many ideas will flow from the getaway. There is something about being removed from the playing field that helps us discover a new play. You really can spend so much time looking at forests that you miss seeing the trees.

At School

Education is an investment, and leaders put money into the bank of learning. They make the time to complete or continue their formal education. Online, in accelerated courses, or in traditional programs, they find a way to gain wisdom along with a degree. Leaders also take advantage of alternate learning sources. They may not have the time or resources to enroll in a degree program at a college or university. But they know that a night course at a local high school or community college could be just the thing to sharpen their skills.

A leader is always intent on learning—no matter how far up the ladder he or she may have climbed. It won't take long for a leader in a new situation to discover that he or she doesn't have all the answers. It may only take the obstinacy or lethargy of a team member or board member to bring them to reality. No matter how many letters you may have after your name, there will likely be a situation that calls for a little more education.

Of course, the leader is first and foremost a student of God's Word. Looking at the lives of Old and New Testament leaders provides a wealth of leadership tips. Sit with Moses as he judges the Israelites and is suddenly interrupted by his father-in-law, Jethro. His advice to delegate responsibilities is worth more than one credit in a college course. Follow Jesus across the landscape of time as He trains His followers to build the Kingdom. You'll learn from every stop along the way. Every lesson, from prayer to preaching, will be a lesson that will help you in Christian leadership.

Are there gaps in your knowledge as a leader? In what areas could you use advice, information, or greater skill?

What will you do to acquire it?

51

BECOMING A
SPIRITUAL LEADER

G reat political leaders have always understood that neither ballots nor bullets alone are sufficient for leading a nation. The real battle is always spiritual.

Is your ministry different?

We pastors, even more than other leaders, must advance on our knees. It's never enough to know management principles and tactics. Neither organizational charts nor goal lists are sufficient to lead Christ's Church. We must be men and women of prayer, grounded in the Word, and steeped in the Spirit. We must be spiritual leaders.

These are difficult days. Our people are frightened. They're seeking comfort, assurance, and direction. They need a strong shepherd who preaches, counsels, directs with godly authority, and leads from the heart. Be that shepherd. Our influence is spiritual, not temporal.

I love to tell the story about two nuns who were delivering medical supplies to a nursing home when their car ran out of gas. They searched the car for a gas can, but could find only a bedpan. The sisters walked half a mile to a gas station, filled the bedpan with fuel, and walked back to the car.

As they were carefully pouring the gas into the tank, a man approached in a pickup truck and slowed to a stop. Marveling at what he thought he was seeing, the man said, "Sisters, I'm not Catholic, but I sure do admire your faith."

Most people admire ministers for their faith and depend on them for their prayers. In these days when the pastor's role is being reshaped faster than a kindergartner with a handful of Silly Putty, we must stake our ground on spiritual leadership.

Here's how to be a leader after God's own heart.

Keep Your Spiritual Life in Tune

Amid the hectic shuffle of a minister's day, the most obvious tasks may be the most easily neglected. If we are to lead on God's behalf, we must know Him intimately. And that requires spending time with Him.

Schedule a daily prayer time in your calendar, and then refuse all interruptions. Read the Word for personal growth not just sermon study. Spend a day alone with God occasionally. Develop an accountability partnership. You can't lead with spiritual authority if you don't have any.

Model Spiritual Leadership to Staff

The meeting is tense. A critical decision must be made. Conflicting ideas have been expressed. As the leader, you have a definite agenda. It's tempting to take control of the meeting and push for your desired resolution.

Don't.

Spiritual leaders seek God's wisdom, even when they think they know the right answer. Break business meetings for prayer. Tell your team, "We need to pray about this issue." Then pray.

Model Spiritual Leadership from the Platform

You've seen them, those bigger-than-life preachers who make themselves the hero of every story. As you listen to some pompous orators describe their leadership achievements, counseling successes, and personal exploits, you wonder how God managed to part the Red Sea without them!

Authentic spiritual leaders are candid about their dependence on God. They remind their people that nothing good happens without prayer. They're open about their shortcomings (without soliciting compliments). They make it clear that whatever victories have been won on their watch have been won by the grace of God.

Talk about Things That Matter

Too many sermons are disconnected from reality. It is easier—and less threatening—to preach about the inner life than about war, raising children, business ethics, or marital conflict. But people don't leave church to ponder the mystery of the Trinity, vital as that doctrine might be. They go home to deal with contentious spouses, stressful jobs, and unsettling headlines. Pastors enhance their spiritual authority by applying God's Word to the challenges that people face right now. Spiritual leaders tackle tough issues because their people do. They have something to say about the world in which they are living—and people respect them for it.

Cultivate Discernment

Authority is one half of spiritual leadership; discernment is the other half. Spiritual authority comes from knowing God and being empowered by Him. Spiritual discernment comes from knowing people, reading circumstances, and anticipating outcomes. Discernment is the ability to sense when to speak, what to do, and whom to trust.

Like authority, the practice of discernment requires intimacy with God. Some leaders receive discernment as a spiritual gift; others must cultivate it. Become a student of people and situations. Cultivate counselors whose wisdom you can mine when needed. And above all, search the mind of God. He has promised wisdom for those who seek it.

The world is looking for leadership—spiritual leadership—now more than ever, and you can provide it. Yet remember that position does not equal power. Being a minister does not make one a spiritual leader. You must get close to God, know His mind and heart, and then represent Him to your people.

Lead with authority. Lead with integrity.

People will follow.

52

LEADING UNDER AUTHORITY

Y ou'll never be a leader until you learn to be a follower.
"No man is an island," wrote poet John Donne. We are
connected to one another. And as leaders, we are connected to
the ultimate Leader, Jesus Christ. In order to lead well, we must first
learn to be under authority—the authority of Christ.

That's a problem for some leaders. They mistakenly believe that
being a strong leader means never taking orders from anyone. In reality,
we are all under authority in many ways. Pastors serve under district
superintendents or bishops. A CEO is amenable to a board of directors.
In order to lead well, we must follow faithfully. And that takes humility.

Leaders gain permission to direct and guide others as they begin
to follow God's leadership in their own lives. "Followership" is not
a blind acceptance, nor is it a sign of personal weakness. Rather, it is
an important character trait for any person who hopes to be effective
in leading others. Here are six characteristics of strong, powerful
followership.

A Follower Is Not Afraid to Fail

Most successes in life come after a failure. Failure is the salt that seasons victory. One university professor I know claims that a student whose grade point average is 3.97 has a far greater appreciation for achievement than does a student whose average is 4.0. It is not until you have fallen that you realize how good it feels to stand up!

Followers learn from the mistakes of their leaders. Observation is often as valuable as instruction. Instruction often comes from watching a leader's plan of attack. Followers learn what does or doesn't work by observing the experiences of entrepreneurial leaders. Some of the greatest lessons are learned during some of the greatest failures. How a leader reacts to setbacks can influence those who follow. And those who follow will keep a keen eye on the underlying reasons for those setbacks.

A Follower Is an Original Thinker

When assigned a task by his or her leader, such a follower will not be content to do it the way it has always been done. He or she will think of a new method for or means of accomplishing the job. It may be as simple as changing the site for a meeting to a restaurant instead of a dull conference room. Effective followers are independent thinkers with an entrepreneurial spirit.

Followers are open to new methods. They aren't shackled to leadership traditions. One of the qualities a follower notices in a leader is the leader's adaptability. More often great leaders set the course. Their penchant for the cutting edge drives them to new ventures—and most often to new victories.

A Follower Seeks Wisdom

Good followers heed the advice given in Proverbs 3:5–6: "Lean not on your own understanding; in all your ways acknowledge him, and he will make your paths straight." Following, then, involves acknowledging areas of ignorance or weakness and seeking the wisdom of better-trained people to fill in those gaps.

Followers are information seekers. They take advantage of twenty-first-century media. They look, listen, and reflect. They are readers—and retainers. They take notes. They file ideas. They are always on the lookout for a better method to accomplish their ministry purpose.

A Follower Is One Who Obeys Instruction

Sometimes the word *meekness* is misinterpreted to mean "weakness." That couldn't be further from the truth, for only one who is secure and has strong self-esteem is capable of being truly humble. It takes great inner control to let go of outer control.

Jesus modeled this concept to perfection. The Creator of the family unit learned obedience in the home of His earthly family. The very one who created the forests learned how to work with wood in Joseph's carpenter shop. His greatest sacrifice came at the request of His Heavenly Father. His submission to salvation's plan was an act of willful obedience.

A Follower Is Willing to Do Whatever It Takes to Get the Job Done

It has been said that a person can accomplish much when he or she does not care who gets the credit. An individual is rich when he or she can do the assignments of the poor.

A good follower is willing to give credit to others—including his or her leader. Good followers don't need medals to prove they were faithful in the line of duty. They are willing to pay the price in order to carry out the purpose.

A Follower Knows How to Listen

No one learns anything by talking. All learning is done by listening, watching, or reading. Honest listening is a highly active endeavor, and for a nonlistener it can be a real strain. Taking notes, making eye contact, and summarizing key points are all skills of a good listener—and of a good follower.

Again, Jesus modeled listening. See Him sitting with Nicodemus or the rich young man. Watch Him as He listens to the aching questions of Mary and Martha following the death of their brother. Notice His last actions on the cross, when two thieves "speak their piece." And notice His reaction to pleas of the penitent thief. He gave the greatest sermons or speeches that were ever uttered. But He also did some of the most important listening ever recorded.

Jesus taught us that the first will be last and the last first. It seems ironic, but it is true. And it is also true that a good leader must first become a good follower. Learn to follow the Leader, and others will follow you.

53

MANAGING CHANGE

Change agents are usually considered mavericks. They continually color outside the lines and are willing to stretch traditional ideas. Change agents can make others feel uncomfortable. But change agents are vital! Without these fearsome leaders, no church or organization could grow, improve, or revitalize itself.

Will you be an agent of change? I know it's uncomfortable. It would be easier to accept the status quo, work for the paycheck, and go home at 4:30 every afternoon. But if you're like me, you feel that God is calling us forward toward a new day. You believe that the future always looks brighter than the past and that the best is yet to be. You have a hankering to make that bright future a reality.

It takes no skill to start an avalanche. Anyone can release a torrent of pent up energy, perhaps even by accident. It isn't difficult to initiate change. Managing change? That's a different story. It takes a highly skilled leader to manage the process of change effectively. Here are six critical skills for change management. Master them, and you will prevent your change from generating an avalanche of angry criticism.

Enlighten Others

All changes begin with a period of enlightenment, a growth in understanding. Throughout the Bible, we see how enlightenment took place before any change was realized. Job's understanding of God's sovereignty helped him begin the process of spiritual growth. Nehemiah was enlightened about the ruined condition of Jerusalem's walls before launching his rebuilding campaign.

Begin the process of change by enlightening yourself and others about the current situation and the steps that will be needed to bring about a preferred future.

Create a Sense of Urgency

After the period of enlightenment, others will come to see the need for changes in your ministry or organization. Maximize momentum by creating a sense of urgency around the needed change. Let that sense of urgency drive your team toward the goal. If the team feels that change is not merely useful but imperative, they will be much more likely to accept the cost of change.

Generate a Team Orientation

You can't bring about change by yourself, no matter how tireless or determined you may be. It takes a team effort to make significant change in any organization. Gather a team to discuss the need and generate ideas. Get buy in from as many leaders as you can. It is important that as many constituents as possible become part of the change process. Those who are not involved in the change may become change resisters.

Engage in Strategic Planning

The next skill is strategic planning. Howard Hendricks wrote about his boyhood visits to a park to watch some older men play checkers. On one occasion, one of the men asked Howard if he would like to play. He took the challenge and sat down across from the older man. At first, young Hendricks did well and even captured a few of the older man's checkers. But all of the sudden, the older man picked up one of his checkers, skipped it clear across the board and exclaimed, "King me!" The older man had a plan.

Your change will not succeed without a clear, achievable plan. Energy and momentum will carry you only so far. To create lasting change, you must have a sustainable plan. As you begin the process of change, you must have its end in mind.

Anticipate Needs

What will be the cost of your change? How much funding will be required? How much manpower? How much time? These elements form what is sometimes called the *iron triangle* of change management: money, manpower, and time. If you are short on one, you must be long on another. No change can be accomplished without adequate resources. Factor needed resources into your change management plan. Anticipate the obstacles you will encounter and the resources you will need to overcome them. If you do not plan for these needs, you plan to fail.

Evaluate Progress

Evaluation is the final step in leading change. Three areas must be evaluated in every change management effort: effectiveness, performance and ownership. The effectiveness of a change is evaluated first because it gets at the goal. This evaluation asks, "Are we on target?" *Performance* evaluation asks, "Does the team understand what is expected of them and are they able to do it?" If your staff cannot carry out the plan, the plan is not right for you. *Ownership* evaluation asks, "Have the people bought in to this plan?" A change that is owned by just the leader, or just the leadership team, is unlikely to become reality. When the entire group accepts the change at the outset, it can hardly fail.

Starting change? That's easy. Anyone can upset an apple cart. Managing change effectively requires these six critical skills. Master them, and you will master the art of change.

54

MANAGING RISK

The greatest challenge in the life of any leader comes not from critics or competitors but from within. When faced with a decision, each of us is likely to have two internal voices competing for our attention. One of them says, "It's too risky." The other says, "It's worth the risk." Great leaders are those who have learned to shut out the voices of negativity and self-doubt and to focus on a positive, hopeful vision of the future.

What is the challenge your organization now faces? What are the personal challenges for you as a leader? It's likely that you can achieve more than you ever thought possible if you can free yourself from negative thinking and dare to dream. That is especially true when the rivers of management aren't flowing smoothly.

"If you don't want to run with the big dogs, then stay on the porch." Whoever coined that saying understood this tenet of leadership: It's risky. Every path to opportunity has a few speed bumps. Plans fail. Finances become tight. Markets change. Allies desert you. But great leaders succeed anyway. They have learned to accept risk, bounce back from failure, and continue working toward a goal.

Life doesn't come with a money-back guarantee, and neither does a dream. If you are to pursue yours, you'll have to take some risks. Every successful venture had a risk factor. Someone dared to inch their way out onto the farthest end of the limb. Someone dared to trust God's power rather than human might—or fright.

How will you know that the risks are worth taking? These questions will help you evaluate the advisability of any endeavor:

What Is the Worst That Could Happen?

The worst probably won't happen, but you must be prepared in case it does. As an entrepreneur, you must be prepared to lose your entire investment; it could happen. If your goal is to conquer Mount Everest, you must be prepared to lose your life; some have. If you can't accept the worst possible outcome, the risk is too great. When you know what you're willing to lose, you know what you can afford to risk.

Like it or not, Murphy's Law is here to stay. For many reasons—including carnal cohorts—there is a trap door along the journey. That trap may or may not open, but it's worth considering that it may. That isn't negative thinking; rather, it is positive planning.

What Will Most Likely Happen?

Most leaders who fail do so because they overestimate the possibility of success and underestimate the possibility of failure. Ask hard questions about your plan before you begin. How realistic are the goals? How reliable is the data you're using? Who has tried this venture before, and with what result? What are the pitfalls, and what will we do to avoid them?

This question is harder to answer because the future cannot be known. But if you can determine, for instance, that your plan has a 75 percent chance of success, you may be more willing to risk your time or other assets. It's up to you to put the plan together (with the guidance of the Holy Spirit). There are enough examples in Christian leadership to allow you to put a reasonable game plan in place. The successes and failures are well-known. From them you may conclude that A plus B will most likely result in C.

What Is My Contingency Plan?

Even if the worst doesn't happen, something unexpected probably will. What "relief effort" have you included in your leadership manual? How will you respond if you lose your funding? What will happen if you miss your first quarter goals? Who can fill in if a key player becomes ill? If you don't plan to deal with a crisis, a crisis will deal with you.

Almost every building project has a "What if?" included. It's your job as a Christian leader to look for it in the plans. And then plan for it in the event that it solidifies—like paw prints in cement.

What's the alternate source of funding? Who can I turn to if a team member drops out? How will my ministry plan change if my ministry base shifts? Who can provide mentoring in a crisis situation? What is my Plan B?

Charles Lindbergh said, "Life without risk is not worth living." He knew that to succeed in anything, you must be willing to dare. But undertaking risk for its own sake is foolish. When you know what might happen, know what you will do about it, and know how much you're willing to lose, you can learn to evaluate risk effectively.

It's worth the risk.

55

LEADING IN UNCERTAIN TIMES

In church leadership, one minute you may be the guest of honor at the head table, and the next minute you may be shown the door! Misunderstandings, missteps, and miscommunications can make leadership a dangerous construction zone.

You should get a merit badge for learning to deal with adversity, but you probably won't. You'll just get another set of marching orders for another problem that needs your attention, another situation that calls for all the tact, wisdom, and patience that you can squeeze out of that last nerve.

But you can do it! That's why He called you and appointed you to the leadership position you now hold. You are needed for just such a time as this!

Jibe is a sailing term. It means to change a vessel's course when sailing with the wind so that the boom swings to the opposite side. Any weekend sailor knows the feeling of having to make a sudden turn in order to catch the changing direction of the wind.

Then the turmoil begins!

The sailor learns in a hurry that when it comes to being on the water, "duck" isn't just a waterfowl. When the skipper yells "Coming about!" he really means, "Duck! You're about to get clobbered!"

As a leader, have you ever been caught in the winds of a sudden jibe?

The good news is that the winds of adversity often cause a positive updraft: People start communicating, ideas are batted about, solutions begin to surface, and hidden agendas are posted.

The vibrant leader learns to make good use of the jibes. He or she learns to use adversity to advantage, and the ship sails on. Here are some "sailing tips."

Pray First

The Christian leader should consider prayer a first resort. It's not the last item on their to-do list, it's the first. Often when adversity comes, the leader is in such a weakened spiritual state that it affects every attitude or action that follows.

Check Your Heart

When David prayed, "Search me O God," he was in a leadership role. It's a good example for every Christian leader. Be open to the checks and balances of the Spirit. Leaders aren't always right—or wrong. But leaders are quick to acknowledge their human weaknesses. Are there areas of your life that could be feeding the fire? Is there something you can do to put out the flames? The Holy Spirit is faithful to lead the heart that wants leadership.

Be Proactive

Adversity is often the result of lethargy. Someone has let down their guard. Someone has failed to take proper initiative. Decisive actions don't need to be quick decisions; they just need to be solid.

Accept Change

When a leader has a "my way or the highway" attitude, the "led" often choose the highway. A willingness to make personal sacrifices for the greater cause of the Kingdom is a mark of true leadership.

And some of those sacrifices will include the "C" word. When the winds suddenly shift, when unexpected change occurs, it will take every personal effort to keep the boat afloat—including either trying new things or remodeling the old.

Keep it Positive

Faith works best under fire. It reflects the fragrance of Christ even in a field of weeds. A steady smile. A warm greeting. An honest affirmation. A genuine respect for others. There are positive ways to turn the negative into the positive.

Course corrections are common for those who desire to excel.

On September 11, 2001, the sudden and horrible winds of adversity changed the course of almost everyone's journey. Hearts needed encouragement. Hope needed to be raised like a banner over the burning rubble of a nation blindsided by an explosion of uncontrollable anger. Churches and their leaders rushed to help, using the very adversity to preach the advantages of faith.

Adversity brought sudden attention to the core mission. Churches were soon filled with seeking hearts, and pastors and teachers had a message already in place. Instead of succumbing to the events, Christian workers rose to the occasion, giving cups of cold water, counseling the grief stricken and fearful, turning their energies to rebuilding shattered lives, sharing resources with those who had suffered setbacks.

Adversity is a wake-up call for leaders. Bend to it, and your life will be filled with anxiety and ineffectiveness. Adjust to it, and you can thrive, even in the worst of times.

PART 5

COACHING

Lord, make me a crisis man. Let me not be a milepost on
a single road, but make me a fork that men must turn
one way or another in facing Christ in me.

—JIM ELIOT

We proclaim him, admonishing and teaching everyone
with all wisdom, so that we may present everyone perfect
in Christ. To this end I labor, struggling with all his energy,
which so powerfully works in me.

—COLOSSIANS 1:28–29

56

ENLISTING OTHERS
TO ACHIEVE THE VISION

Have you ever sat in a car with the emergency flashers on, waiting for someone to bring you a tank of gas? I have. It's one of the loneliest places on earth. It's not just the inconvenience to your rescuer; it's the embarrassment of their seeing that you didn't calculate enough resources for the trip.

Many leaders run on so little gas they would short-circuit the low-fuel light on any dashboard. But loss of strength isn't the only issue. Leaders also fall short on quality time with their loved ones and friends. They often miss out on times of rest and relaxation. They often suffer burnout or subject themselves to temptations they would otherwise be strong enough to resist.

There has to be a way to move an organization forward without its leader falling behind. Leaders must understand that God has gifted others with skills that need to be refined and released in the community of faith.

Leadership isn't about making a one-time impression or achieving a one-time goal. It's about eternity. It's about making a difference for Christ and His Church. How? By accomplishing a mission through the involvement of others.

In order to be successful over the long haul, leaders must avoid the trap of doing more and must learn to do fewer things more effectively. I suggest a 3-D approach: designate, delegate, and dissociate—three-dimensional leadership.

Designate

Everything you do in the Kingdom is important. But not everything needs to be done at the same time. In real estate, it's location. In management, it's delegation. Every leader needs to assign a priority level to his or her work. Almost every management system recommends the practice, but it is often ignored. Whether you use A-B-C files, marked file drawers, or PDA programs, somehow you must avoid lumping all work together on the same desktop. Designate it!

Priority One Is for Items That Need Immediate Attention. This is work that will jeopardize your effectiveness if not completed. It may be a calendar that needs to be completed, a committee that needs to be formed, an e-mail that needs to be sent, and more importantly an evening out with your spouse or family. It is the essential item.

Priority Two Is for Work That Needs Attention in the Near Future. These things must be done, but there is less urgency about them. Personal retreat time, research for a writing project, or dinner with an associate. They are essential activities but not priorities.

Priority Three Is for Work That Is of Some Value but Not Vital. It's any item that you'd like to accomplish but which will not affect your mission if not completed. It may be registration for a night class to improve a hobby skill, it may be a tour of some colleague's new facilities, or it may be the cataloging of books in your personal library. The sun won't stand still if it's not the first item on your daily agenda, but at least it's on your agenda.

When you've designated your tasks as Priority One, Two, or Three, you'll still have the same amount of work to do. But because it is prioritized, you'll be more effective.

Delegate

Determine which of your tasks could be shared by another. As a leader, you must be willing to involve others in your work. Your true task, after all, is to develop and direct others in accomplishing Kingdom priorities. And when you involve others in your work, there is a hidden benefit: They become free to use the gifts God has given them. The added blessing is the relational time you will spend with them—helping them to understand your vision for ministry, and your availability as a friend and mentor.

But to delegate effectively, you must transfer ownership of the task, communicate clear expectations, negotiate a deadline for completion, and reward results appropriately.

Dissociate

Now comes the hard part: relax. When you have delegated properly, things will function as well—and probably better—than if you retained total control. For your own sake, learn to allow your subordinates and coworkers freedom to use their trained skills. Allow them to be both creative and responsible for results. By doing so, they'll grow, the organization will grow, and you'll be free to do other things.

If you're an effective leader, you will constantly have more ideas than you can possibly pursue. The heart and mind of a leader are continually pursuing a path of ministry excellence. How do you maintain both peak efficiency and a survivable pace? Designate, delegate, and dissociate.

Master the three Ds, and you'll succeed for the long haul.

57

INSPIRING OTHERS
TO SUCCEED

There she stood in the line at the post office, a line that wound its way almost out the front door. A fellow customer spoke to the elderly lady waiting to buy some stamps. "Ma'am, you must be very tired. Did you know there's a stamp machine over there in the corner?" He pointed to the machine built into the wall.

"Why, yes, thank you," the lady replied, "but I'll just wait here a little while longer. I'm getting close to the window."

The customer became insistent. "But it would be so much easier for you to avoid this long line and buy your stamps from the machine."

The woman patted him on the arm and answered, "Oh, I know. But that old machine would never ask me how my grandchildren are doing."

Leaders would be well-advised to spend less time on the organizational machinery and more time on the people within the organization. Remember, people will not sweat, invest, or risk for an organization. But they will stretch beyond themselves for human connections.

People first!

Rocket ships are not built by superheroes. They're built by ordinary people who have been given the right training, skills, and equipment to do the job. Leaders are the ones who bring the people and resources together to accomplish something extraordinary.

Leaders accomplish their work through others. That means a primary task of every leader is to bring out the best in those around them, inspiring others to reach beyond themselves. Leaders equip, motivate, and direct the work of their teams.

Here are some thoughts on how to inspire others to reach for the stars.

Focus on Your Team's Spiritual Growth

Leaders aren't just managers. They are shepherds as well. Any effort to spur the spiritual growth of the leadership team is time more than well spent! Your team is on a spiritual journey—not just an organizational trek. They need guidance. They need pastoral counseling, biblical training, and skills evaluation.

Connect Weaker Members with Stronger Ones

Barnabas was a great encourager in the New Testament church. But even he needed a backup. He knew that another member of his home team had strengths that were needed for his work. "Then Barnabas went to Tarsus to look for Saul, and when he found him, he brought him to Antioch" (Acts 11:25–26).

One effective way to train leaders is through apprenticeship, linking beginners with veterans. Leadership skills are like germs; hang around people who have them, and pretty soon you'll have them too!

Make a Long-Term Commitment to the Team

Team members want to know whether the leader is committed for the long haul. Of course, your "tour of duty" depends on the leading of the Holy Spirit, but your team must sense that you are there for the duration. Short-term commitments short-circuit team efforts. For an entire year, Barnabas and Saul met with the church in Antioch and taught a great number of people. In fact, it was in that city that the disciples were first called "Christians." The long-term commitment of those leaders paid off in triumph. The followers of a religion became followers of Christ!

Stick with your team. Your commitment will do more than rub off on them; it will inspire them.

Keep Looking Up

Every team gets down from time to time. When that happens, the leader's attitude can make or break the situation. Inspiring leaders keep looking up. Inspiring spiritual leaders have a firm grasp on the promises and power of God. They're students of the Word. They're worshippers. They're readers of good leadership books.

Inspiring leaders have bought in to the Great Commission, the Great Commandment, and the Great Commitment ("I am the vine; you are the branches. If a man remains in me and I in him, he will bear much fruit; apart from me you can do nothing" John 15:5). They keep the focus positive, always looking for a way to turn advantage out of adversity. Sometimes the quarterback must become the cheerleader, rallying the team to keep going.

Expect the Best

Most teams perform up or down to the expectations placed on them. If a leader accepts excuses, or—worse yet—makes them, the team will never reach its full potential. People achieve greatness only when someone demands it from them. A great leader always expects the best.

Take a good look at your team members. They are ordinary men and women, that's true. But they can do extraordinary things if the right leader equips, motivates, and guides them to victory.

58

BECOMING A LEADER WHO INSPIRES CONFIDENCE

I f you've ever watched a NASCAR race, you'll know that racing engines push the limits of performance. (So do Christian leaders.) It takes a highly tuned engine to turn more than 9,000 RPMs and produce up to 800 horsepower. And it takes a highly tuned leader to face the demands of this age.

Leaders cannot navigate this high-stress world without a high-performance engine—that is, a heart that is fully devoted to Jesus Christ and fully committed to keep body, soul, and mind in shape. If we are to lead the pack, then we must follow the Leader. That will require regular preventative maintenance in the form of self-examination, time spent in prayer, and the practice of accountability.

In racing, fine-tuning often makes the difference between reaching the finish line and the finished line. What's true on the track is true in the world. As leaders, we need to keep our spiritual lives in perfect adjustment. Here are some tips on living for Christ in a society that often seems like it's going around in circles.

Stay Spiritually Alert

Start your day with a "team meeting." What an awesome privilege to face the day with the realization that you've met with the Father, the Son, and the Holy Spirit! God has something to say about each activity of your day. Read His Word. The Bible really is a light for our path. The age-old saying "seven days without the Bible makes one weak" is true. Stay alert with a heart filled with God's truth.

Talk to God in prayer before you talk to anyone else. You can hit the floor running on eight cylinders of heavenly power. Praise Him for the night's rest (even if you missed some sleep). Praise Him for His promised presence and power for the day's activities. Praise Him for your family and friends. And praise Him for putting enough confidence in you that He would assign you the responsibility of helping to build His kingdom on earth.

Of course, that won't be your only meeting. You can pray on your knees and you can pray on your feet—running. Constant communication with heaven's headquarters will give you added wisdom and strength for the day. There is no substitute for prayer and Bible study!

Focus on the Future

A New Testament veteran gave this worthy example: "Forgetting what is behind and straining toward what is ahead, I press on toward the goal to win the prize for which God has called me heavenward in Christ Jesus" (Phil. 3:13–14). The Apostle Paul knew that ultimate victory belongs to the faithful, not the fearful. Throwing pity parties for past mistakes only spins your wheels.

If you want a high-performance heart, focus on the future. When your past is forgiven, it's forgotten. The enemy of your faith, the devil, is a great historian. He delights in displaying the past on the message board of your heart. Don't let him. Jesus is a futurist not a historian. He forgave your past so that you might have a bright future.

Give Yourself Away

We like to hoard things. When we get a little money, status, power, or affirmation, we usually keep it for ourselves. When you come to the conclusion that you gain most by giving, you will have a head start on a lot of folks who call themselves Christian. Where to start: the offering plate. Begin with the tithe and go from there. Your ten percent isn't really yours; it's God's. The checkbook is one of the first places to look if the blessings aren't flowing.

Be willing to give yourself away in service to others. Ministry doesn't always happen on the platform or at the head of the table in the boardroom. Ministry often happens in the backyard of a shut-in, helping him or her rake leaves. Ministry sometimes takes an extra trip to the supermarket for some groceries that will feed a family of new immigrants. Generosity is the mark of a winner—at work, at home, and everywhere in life.

Guard Your Eyes

In our Ken-and-Barbie world, the Madison Avenue mavens know that sex sells. But it's also a buyer! Loveless, vow-less sex always takes; it never gives the intimacy that it promises. It is void of God's original intent for human sexual fulfillment.

That's why high-performance hearts steer clear of alluring looks and inviting glances. Godly leaders have made a deal with their eyes— they refuse to look at images that have only a sexual intent. They say no when others say yes.

High-performance hearts also have control over their computers. They don't linger in chat rooms that offer opportunities to engage in harmful conversations with the opposite sex. They don't visit Web sites that are porn driven. They are wise to the ways of a world that seeks to keep them in spiritual—and financial—bondage. They protect their marriage by protecting their hearts.

Keep the Faith

Occasionally, a mighty racing machine may be seen at the close of a great race putting along like a pachyderm with a sprained ankle. The pole sitter winds up pooped. Why? He ran out of fuel.

A lot of life's pole sitters have finished the same way. Their character didn't have the right mix of courage and determination. They ran too hard for too long, neglecting the spiritual life. Great leaders avoid that trap. They commit their entire lives to completing their God-given task.

Winners make the commitment to go all the way. They plan to spend quality time with the Lord. They plan to manage stress and anger. They pay attention to their physical health. They spend money wisely. Make the right decisions with your time, money, and attention and you'll be a fruitful leader for years to come.

59

ORCHESTRATING THE WORK OF OTHERS

Aworker is responsible for one thing. A leader is responsible for everything. Leaders are skilled at managing a myriad of details. The most successful leaders are always the best organized. Day planners, PERT charts, and BlackBerrys are not gimmicks or gadgets. They are the tools of the trade for a successful leader. If you can track and control the work of many people, you will multiply your effectiveness— and see greater results.

Ministers not only rise and fall on their preaching or teaching skills, they also must be well organized. Twenty-first-century administration makes high demands of the ministry professional. Beyond sharing a devotional thought, preaching skills aren't that important in a board meeting or a church conference. Ministers need more. They need to get a handle on putting handles on plans or projects. They need to provide structure to an organization— a strong enough structure that will keep it standing when the winds of adversity begin to blow.

Organization comes naturally to some, while others struggle to gather enough resources to put a one-table picnic together. I suggest that even the unorganized can become organized. There are several important steps in the transition.

Know Where to Go

No person responsible for the success of an entire organization can keep all the important information in his or her head. But they can keep it at their fingertips. Leaders can have a lousy memory as long as they can remember one thing—where to look for the answer. Data management systems, filing systems, and ruthlessly organized assistants are a leader's best friends. Create a system for organizing information, and make it work.

Data management is ever evolving. We've come from the pad and pencil to the PDA. Administrators have made the leap from walls full of file cabinets to computer hard drives filled with facts and figures. Granted, some have been dragged kicking and screaming into the Internet age, but once they get their technical feet wet they're more than happy to dive in. Electric typewriters have become as obsolete as carbon paper. And managers who refuse to utilize new technologies can quickly become part of the dinosaur age.

You've probably made the leap. You've joined the battery-burning age. But in case you haven't made the jump, remember that there are those within your church or organization who have. Find them, orient them, and then use them for God's glory and building His kingdom.

Make a Plan

It's tried and true: If you fail to plan, you plan to fail. Leaders who begin the day, week, or year without carefully crafted goals and objectives will finish exactly where they started—nowhere.

List the goals for your life and prioritize them. Do the same for the year.

Make a task list for each day. Don't attack your ambition without a strategy. Plan to succeed.

There is a terrific opportunity awaiting you. There's a cabin in the mountains, a room near the ocean, or a stump in the heart of a forest. There is a place just waiting for you to inhabit, along with your Bible, your planner, and your pen or recorder. It's the planning retreat. It's the place where you can put your dreams into motion. It's a place where the Holy Spirit can fill your heart and mind with a vision to make bold spiritual and organizational moves.

You don't have time to get alone with God for times of planning? Make time. Plug that planning moment into your calendar. You wouldn't build a skyscraper without blueprints, so why try to help with Kingdom-building without a plan. Jesus proved He was the greatest organizer of all time by accomplishing the entire mission that His Father gave Him—in just thirty-six months. No wonder He spent those extended hours on the mountain praying!

Work the Plan

Many leaders begin the day with good intentions but are quickly pulled off track by distractions or problems. The phone rings. An e-mail pops into view. A colleague drops in to discuss some issues. Suddenly the day is gone.

Take it back! Once you've planned your time, work the plan. Say no to any distraction except critical emergencies. Most of the "urgent" tasks that interrupt your day are probably unimportant. Ignore them. Stick to the plan.

Harness Others

In the old days, farmers plowed by yoking two oxen together. Tied side by side, they had no choice but to pull together. Good leaders are able to harness the energy of others, organizing their labor to greatest advantage. They control not only their own time but also the time and efficiency of their teammates. Good leaders are able to organize others without becoming taskmasters.

Someone you know is waiting to learn some of the things you know. You are not only a pastor, you are a teacher—a mentor whose mission is to transfer bits and bytes of knowledge into the lives of future leaders. Start now. Form a learning center in your church or organization, whether it is a classroom in the Christian education facility or a booth at Starbucks. Let God lead you to that person who has the potential for leader greatness, and start investing.

Organization is not only necessary for multitasking, it's a defining quality for successful leadership. Modern managers must be skilled at knowing how to find information, manage resources, and harness the energy of others.

Leaders create structure—through which power flows.

60

QUALITIES OF
A MENTOR

No other first-century figure modeled leadership like the Apostle Paul. Perhaps his most important leadership quality was his focus on leading *people* rather than *organizations*. The organization of the first-century church was carried on the very human shoulders of inspired people who were recruited, strengthened in their faith, and disciplined in ministry skills by other leaders. The bottom line is this: Leadership is influence.

Paul, the Mentor

Paul knew how to train leaders by pouring his love for the Lord into their hearts and minds. He taught them about spiritual priorities as well as leadership qualities. They, in turn, used his words to teach others. They used his life as a lesson in Christian greatness. The principles he so effectively modeled can be applied in every denominational or local church setting.

One of Paul's most effective leadership methods was mentoring. Before Timothy became a great pastor in the New Testament church, he was a great pupil—a pupil of his mentor, Paul the apostle. Paul knew the principle of leadership multiplication. Following the example of the Galilean, the apostle knew he could catch more fish by teaching others to fish than by casting his solitary line into a multitude of spiritual fishing holes.

The postmodern church needs Christian leadership that will invest itself in the lives of others—who will then show others by word and deed how to excel in life and ministry. The leadership commission of the apostle hasn't been nullified. "And the things you have heard me say in the presence of many witnesses entrust to reliable men who will also be qualified to teach others" (2 Tim. 2:2). We have a continuing mandate to mobilize leaders to reach the lost, equip the believers, and encourage the church. Mentoring is a tried and proven method for accomplishing that task.

A Definition of Mentoring

What is a mentor? A mentor is a godly leader/coach who has committed time and energy to sharing personal growth and ministerial and administrative skills with a spiritual son or daughter—a believer who has obvious spiritual gifts and a teachable spirit. The process is best exemplified in the relationship between the Apostle Paul and his son in the faith, Timothy. "Timothy, my son, I give you this instruction in keeping with the prophecies once made about you, so that by following them you may fight the good fight" (1 Tim. 1:18).

The task of attracting and mentoring future leaders lies in your hands. Who are the best candidates for mentoring? Look for someone in your church or organization with obvious leadership skills. The person may not currently have a prominent position. Perhaps he or she has few platform or boardroom skills. But when assigned a task and a crew of volunteers, he or she accomplishes stated goals with ease and unity.

I've discovered seven basic principles for effective mentoring.

Knowledge Combined with Experience Is the Best Mentoring Process

"What you heard from me, keep as the pattern of sound teaching, with faith and love in Christ Jesus" (2 Tim. 1:13). An effective mentor encourages potential leaders by patiently leading them through ongoing, on-the-job learning experiences. Jesus learned in the Temple by listening to the Jewish teachers, and in the carpenter shop by watching His skilled foster father, Joseph. The most effective mix is a combination of formal training and informal learning experiences.

A Leader's Personal Life Is the Greatest Lesson

The development of exemplary leaders comes by modeling exemplary leadership. The *how* is best taught by a trusted *who*! Paul reminded Timothy, "I thank God, whom I serve, as my forefathers did" (2 Tim. 1:3). Someone modeled the lifestyle that Paul fleshed out in the lives of others.

Mentors Are Lifters

Great leaders make everyone feel worthwhile. Timothy learned about encouragement from Paul while on the job. "We sent Timothy, who is our brother and God's fellow worker in spreading the gospel of Christ, to strengthen and encourage you in your faith" (1 Thess. 3:2). Encouragement is a vital ingredient in the mentoring process. Sending a note or e-mail, making a quick phone call, stopping in and letting your student know "out loud" that you appreciate his or her efforts are just a few of the ways a mentor can make an investment in future leaders.

Mentors Need Strong Shoulders and Listening Ears

Paul reminded the church at Corinth about his constant and compassionate concern for them. "I face daily the pressure of my concern for all the churches," he wrote (2 Cor. 11:28). Who brought out your best qualities? Probably someone who focused on you. Someone who had a strong shoulder to lean on and who would listen when it seemed like no one else even heard you.

Mentors Are Transparent

Paul wasn't afraid to share his tragedies as well as his triumphs. "You, however, know all about my teaching, my way of life, my purpose, faith, patience, love, endurance, persecutions, sufferings . . . Yet the Lord rescued me from all of them" (2 Tim. 3:10–11). Rose-colored glasses will not help leader recruits see better. They need to understand that the fields "white unto harvest" have some weeds!

Mentors Are Guardians

"Timothy, guard what has been entrusted to your care" (1 Tim. 6:20). Even as Paul taught that truth, he understood the weight of his own guardianship. Mentors will do their share of groaning under the weight of possibilities for their charges. They also delight in understanding the faithfulness of their Lord. They seek to combine intercession with instruction in the power of the Holy Spirit.

One of the leader's greatest privileges is to duplicate his or her ministry through the life of another. In fact, mentoring is one of the highest forms of ministry.

61

TAKING RESPONSIBILITY
FOR YOUR MINISTRY

"The price of greatness is responsibility," said Winston Churchill, and it's true. Great leaders act responsibly. They don't need to be told when they're wrong. More often than not, they'll tell you. They demonstrate in their own lives the personal openness and honesty they expect from their team or their fellow parishioners.

Leaders Take Responsibility for Their Performance

Leaders don't become defensive when they miss the mark. They don't tear up their credentials when their sermons bomb. They don't resign after every troubling board meeting. They don't spend their nights fretting about their days. They just go on.

They realize that too many other things are at stake to worry about saving face. The team member who spends an inordinate amount of time reflecting on the last play is the one who probably won't execute the next one. A good leader is willing to say, "That one was my fault; now let's get on with it."

Leaders Take Responsibility for Their Attitudes

They're willing to move down the checklist of motivations to see if they're hurting morale by being critical, demanding, or selfish. They don't want to be the sand that keeps the machine from running smoothly. They are willing to make an ego adjustment for the good of the church.

They learn how to look at their people through their own mirror. They realize that the most irritating characteristics of others either lie dormant within them or have already blossomed. Great leaders profess to be too weak to carry grudges.

Leaders Take Responsibility for Their Personal Lives

Great leaders don't try to separate character from career or ethics from excellence. They live from five to nine the same way they live from nine to five. They have integrity. "I was wrong." "I'm sorry." The sentences are rather small, but they are highly significant to them. Great leaders don't hesitate to say them when needed.

Leaders Take Responsibility for Their Ministries

They don't try to gloss over their faults. They don't blame the sound technician for missing a cue from the bulletin. They don't point fingers at less-than-musical special songs. They don't hide their fears under the stones of arrogance or pride.

Leaders Take Responsibility for Their Families

Many leaders have experienced life in a glass house. Many of them have heard the criticisms heaped on themselves and their spouses. So they do all that they possibly can to keep their children from the hurts that they have felt personally.

Great leaders have learned to be defenders of their family. They don't excuse the wrong actions or attitudes of their family members, but they refuse to allow critics to squeeze the very life out of them. They teach their family by the lessons they have learned in leadership.

Leaders Take Responsibility for Their Teams

They know that a chain is only as strong as its weakest link and that a caravan never moves faster than the slowest camel. When those around them have performance problems, they are quick to notice and offer solutions. The best leaders never ask, "What's wrong with you?" but always, "How can we do better?"

Great leaders stand between their team and the crowd. They are always ready to defend their team's honest and best attempt—even when it falls far short of perfection. They are willing to take the hits for the team. Willing to face their accusers with the team. Willing to go out on a limb at a business meeting if it means salvaging a life or a career.

Leaders Take Responsibility for Results

Their church may have missed the attendance goal by one hundred. Their church may be thousands of dollars short in meeting their fund-raising goal. But you'll never hear them say, "My team let me down," "I could have, if only . . . ," or "It wasn't my fault." Great leaders know that the buck always stops with them. They don't point fingers or assign blame; they accept results and keep moving.

William Arthur Ward said, "God gives us the ingredients for our daily bread, but He expects us to do the baking." Great leaders are the people with their sleeves rolled up, kneading the dough. They have been given a responsibility, and they live up to it.

Great leaders leave great legacies. They teach by example. They preach through their failures. They point to the Cross instead of to themselves. They bring the very best out of the very worst by giving them room to grow beyond who they are. They reach for the stars and never blame the clouds for dimming their view.

Great leaders are a lot like Christ.

62

TEAM-BUILDING TIPS

Amerian humorist and writer Kin Hubbard once said, "The safe way to double your money is to fold it over once and put it in your pocket." That may (or may not) be good financial advice, but in leadership circles, the best way to double your productivity and influence is by teaming up with others.

One Super Bowl–winning coach answered the question of a curious reporter about the coach's great success. He said, "I'm an ordinary guy surrounded by extraordinary men."

Throughout history, great leaders have succeeded because they discovered the value of teamwork. The mission you're engaged in is too great to go it alone. You need a solid team of men and women who can grasp your vision, are committed to the mission, and will see it through to the very end.

Whether you are leading a group of two, twenty, or two hundred, the Bible outlines timeless principles for leading your team. Take a look at these tips for leading by the Book.

Start with the Best Team Members

If you were building a professional sports team, you wouldn't seek out second-stringers from the college ranks. You'd go for the first teamers. It's the same in church leadership: Go for the best. Often you will need to recruit the busiest people in your church. Why? If they are qualified and trusted in other areas of their lives, they will likely be qualified for ministry. Good teams start with good team members.

When early church leaders needed personnel, they looked for people who were known to be filled with the Holy Spirit. You won't make progress toward your purpose until you recruit team members who have the right hearts, that is, whose hearts are right with God. Recruit people of character. Never allow expediency to take precedence over integrity. A river that is flowing within its banks has direction and purpose. Be sure all your team members are "in the flow," that they have a common commitment to Christ and are willing to be guided by the Holy Spirit.

Be Available to Your Team

Team members often need help. As someone put it, "Many are called, but a few are frozen." The frozen ones may be people who simply do not know what to do. Perhaps they need assistance in the form of training, a job description, a timeline, or equipment. In other words, they need a leader who will help them become their best for God.

For example, Christian laypeople in the New Testament church of Antioch needed feeding. They were suffering from a deficiency in their spiritual diet. Paul and Barnabas were dispatched to right some doctrinal wrongs. In the same way, you may need to instruct, correct, train, and even rebuke team members from time to time. As a leader, you are a shepherd. And one responsibility of the shepherd is to feed the sheep.

Be a Director for Your Team

In television, the floor director is responsible for the movements of cameras and actors. The director's commands—as relayed from the production booth above—will make the difference in a fine program or a fine mess.

You are the floor director for your team. They're waiting for your cues. They'll need to know the script. They'll need to know how to move in synch. Your instructions will add to the success of their ministries. Cast the vision for them. Hold the goal before them. Position them. Direct them.

Supervise Your Team

Your team will need checks and balances. It will need to know its boundaries as well as its opportunities. Your job as a leader is to lovingly and patiently set those boundaries.

Often the Apostle Paul circled back to visit a church where he had previously ministered. He needed to check on its spiritual condition. He needed to instruct its leaders. That "circling back" is an essential quality of a leader. Quality control is a vital task for any leader. It's one thing to give birth to a team, but it's another thing to raise it. That rearing takes nurturing and supervision. It requires following up as well as leading.

Motivate Your Team

Professionals in industry, education, and science know how important it is to stay on the cutting edge. Your team members need to be there too. Inspire them to be their best. Challenge them to succeed. When they're tired, allow them to rest. Then send them out refreshed.

You are not only a coach; you are a cheerleader. Your team will need to hear your cheers as well as your critiques. They will face lonely battlefields. They need to know that someone is with them—no matter what. That's your job.

There is great triumph in teamwork. What could not be accomplished by one individual can be accomplished by a team.

63

DEFINING SUCCESS IN MINISTRY

How do you measure success?
There are many things that we might use as a yardstick for achievement. Money is one marker. Those who are successful in any endeavor are usually financially blessed. That applies to institutions as well. Growth is another indicator of accomplishment. If we have more attendees, more members, more customers, or a higher enrollment, then we are likely more successful.

Yet, all of these standards of success mean nothing if we are not also successful in spiritual terms. What does it mean for a Christian leader to be successful? Paul gives us the answer: "I want to know Christ and the power of his resurrection and the fellowship of sharing in his sufferings, becoming like him in his death" (Phil. 3:10).

We must determine to be successful leaders in every way. We want to succeed financially. We want to excel in reaching our goals. We want to be effective in advancing Christ's kingdom. But more than that, we want to be men and women who are becoming more like our Master, Jesus Christ.

God isn't a "finders keepers" Father. He is the giver of every good and perfect gift, according to James. His greatest gift was His only Son.

Out of His love for us, God was willing to give His dearest possession on our behalf. He gave, and we reap the eternal benefit.

That same cycle of giving can be realized in our lives in other ways. God promises to supply in response to our service. Remember what Jesus said: "Seek first his kingdom and his righteousness, and all these things will be given to you as well" (Matt. 6:33). Let's look at this and other laws of the harvest to see how they apply to our lives.

We Reap What We Invest

In nature, the harvest comes only after sowing. In football, the touchdown comes after the run or the pass. In science, the discovery comes after the experiment. The effort produces the effect. It's the same in the spiritual realm. The Bible says, "The wicked man earns deceptive wages, but he who sows righteousness reaps a sure reward" (Prov. 11:18).

In God's kingdom, our investments result in expectations. It's a matter of faith. We invest, and then we believe God for the return. And you can be assured that no financial statement on earth will ever reflect a greater return on investment than what we will receive from our Heavenly Father.

Our returns will not always be given in dollars. There are more important things than monetary reward: peace, love, joy, purpose, family, and talents. The list of benefits is nearly endless—but it all starts with our personal investment.

We Reap in God's Time

The wisdom writer said, "There is a time for everything, and a season for every activity under heaven" (Eccl. 3:1). In the human realm, we're often on a predictable financial time clock. We live by quarterly or year-end reports. We circle April 15 on our calendars. We receive paychecks every two weeks.

But God isn't necessarily on the same schedule. He rewards us in "due time." First Peter 5:6 says, "Humble yourselves, therefore, under God's mighty hand, that he may lift you up in due time." God isn't limited by earth's time or space. He looks beyond the immediate to the long range. Throughout history, His prophecies and promises have been given when the time was right—and always right on time.

God knows exactly what you need and when you need it. You may not see an immediate return on some investment of time, talent, or treasure you have made, but it will come along right on schedule—God's schedule. Your job is to keep working and trust the Lord of the harvest.

We Reap More Than We Invest

Jesus illustrated this principle of reaping more than we invest in one of His parables. He told of some seed that fell on good soil, where it produced a crop up to one hundred times what had been sown. (See Matt. 13:8.) God doesn't reward us with just what we deserve or even just enough. He always provides more.

At the end of a sermon on giving, I once promised to give people their money back in ninety days if they found that God didn't bless their tithing. One older man stood up and said, "Pastor, I discovered the joy of giving when I was twenty-five years old—and you can't out-give God!" He then offered a refund to anyone who was unsatisfied after tithing for 180 days! During my seven years of ministry at that church, no one ever claimed the refund.

Heaven hasn't been downsized. God's resources aren't subject to budget cuts. So when you're on the expecting side of a heavenly investment, you can look for a lavish reward. Jesus said, "If you then, though you are evil, know how to give good gifts to your children, how much more will your Father in heaven give the Holy Spirit to those who ask him!" (Luke 11:13).

When you invest with the Savior, your resources are secure. The laws of the harvest are still in effect, and there will be a reward.

64

INSPIRING OTHERS
TO DREAM

S omeone once wrote, "I've dreamed many dreams that never came true. I've seen them vanish at dawn. But I've realized enough of my dreams, thank God, to make me want to dream on."

If you just want an educated explanation, the dictionary says that a dream is a "visionary creation of the imagination," or a "strongly desired goal or purpose." But if you want an educated explanation wrapped in eternal truth, the Word of God says that a dream is "being sure of what we hope for and certain of what we do not see" (Heb. 11:1). (Oh, by the way, that's also called faith!)

As I have observed the life and ministry of my friends through the years, I've noticed that the real survivors were those who dared to dream. They were the faithful who were full of faith. In spite of limitations, oppositions, and even inquisitions, they refused to let go of the plan that God had planted in their hearts.

They Saw a Plan in the Problem

They refused to look at their Mount Everest-like assignments without thinking either of a mountain-climbing expedition or an earthmoving excavation. They refused to look at an empty field without thinking of wheat. They looked at fallen trees and thought about how much lumber it would take to build a temple. They had a good grasp on that little chorus we used to sing on prayer meeting night: "God specializes in things called impossible." That song, "Got Any Rivers" by Oscar C. Eliason, blossomed from the root of God's Word: "But Jesus beheld them, and said unto them, With men this is impossible; but with God all things are possible" (Matt. 19:26 KJV).

They Saw a Path Where No One Had Journeyed

With faith in their plan, they ventured out. Every dare begins with a dream. Everything from electricity to electronic games started with a dream and ended with a dare. Those who have made some of the greatest marks on our lives have suffered some of the greatest bruises. Edison failed before he saw the light. Bell was speechless before he dialed the right number. But these daring inventors forged on. They had no one to follow; they simply led the way—into unknown territory. Old Testament leaders paved the way: "Early in the morning they left for the Desert of Tekoa. As they set out, Jehoshaphat stood and said, 'Listen to me, Judah and people of Jerusalem! Have faith in the LORD your God and you will be upheld; have faith in his prophets and you will be successful'" (2 Chron. 20:20). They had 20/20 vision.

They Refused to Pander to Their Critics

The critics told them that their dreams would fail. It didn't matter. They were going to put them to a test anyway. Their critics didn't understand their dream or their plan. They only looked at the problem. They didn't realize that someone with a dream *and* a dare was willing to risk everything for something better. Those who have made the greatest impact have refused to pander to their critics. They refused to barter their plans in the marketplace. They took the advice Moses gave to Israel in the face of their foes: "Do not be afraid of them; remember well what the LORD your God did to Pharaoh and to all Egypt" (Deut. 7:18).

They Plodded until They Ran

Dreams are usually carried out in small steps. Plodding diligently, and often slowly, starts the momentum that ends in a full-speed run. They realized that small progress was better than no progress. So they kept on going. In spite of obstacles. In spite of stumbles. In spite of weariness. They kept planning and they kept putting their plans into action. Like the psalmist, they stayed the course: "My steps have held to your paths; my feet have not slipped" (Ps. 17:5).

They Saw a Power in the Plan

They were people who connected their dream machine to the power strip of Pentecost. They truly believed that they would receive a current of heavenly energy to accomplish the things God wanted to do in them, through them, and sometimes around them. Plans, paths, and even plodding remain dreams until power—Pentecost power—covers them. And that supernatural power comes from focused praying. New Testament dreamers made the discovery: "After they prayed, the place where they were meeting was shaken. And they were all filled with the Holy Spirit and spoke the word of God boldly" (Acts 4:31).

Everyone, except for that third grade teacher looking at a sleepy student on the back row, likes a dreamer. God-given vision is as contagious as a yawn during a slide presentation of the Holy Land. One study revealed that among church-going people, six out of ten want a pastoral leader with a vision. In fact, the wisdom writer warned, "Where there is no vision, the people perish" (Prov. 29:18 KJV). There is no sustainable life without a forward look.

So, pastoral leader, dream on. Plant your plans in the promises of a God who cannot lie, and certainly will not fail—even when the winds of adversity are blowing at hurricane strength.

Don't worry. If God gave you the plan, He'll put the power in it!

65

INSPIRING OTHERS
TO FOLLOW

French naturalist Jean Henri Fabre once conducted an experiment with processionary caterpillars. Processionary caterpillars travel together as a unit, each one joined to the one in front of it. The leader then lays down a silk path as he walks that each caterpillar after him adds to. Fabre induced the caterpillars to climb the side of a pot in his greenhouse. Once he had enough of them to make a complete circle around the rim, he cut off the line. Suddenly the caterpillars had no leader. Each one simply followed the fellow in front of him.

Fabre observed the line for several days, expecting the caterpillars to realize that they needed food and rest, that they needed to deviate from their silk path. But they never did. They just plodded along, following blindly until they fell over, victims of weather, starvation, and exhaustion.

Pastor, you must be the leader in your congregation. By themselves, your church members will have no ambition to "break ranks" and reach into the community, winning souls for Christ. They need you to sense the urgency, set the direction, and guide the way. They need you to *lead*.

You cannot lead people from behind. You can drive them, but they will never follow you. Your leadership will cause resentment.

You cannot lead people from the center. You can comfort or sympathize with them, but they will not respect you as a leader.

You must lead from the front. Only when you are ahead of others can you draw them along with you. That's leadership.

Leadership is attracting people to a cause greater than themselves and motivating them to reach their potential in achieving it. To "attract people" requires you to draw others along with you. To attract people "to a cause" means that you must know where you are going. To attract others to a cause "greater than themselves" means that you must have a sense of urgency about the goal.

Here are seven vital tools for any leader who hopes to attract others to the mission.

Give People the Freedom to Create

People must have freedom to try new things, to be innovative. As a leader, you must release them to explore. "My way or the highway" is a motto for disaster.

But what if they fail? Failure goes with the territory of creativity. Followers need to know that failure is not fatal. Conformity kills. Initiative wins. Free your people to achieve.

Give People Authority, Not Just Responsibility

Effective leaders are not micromanagers. They know how to give associates the authority to make decisions within their area of responsibility. Giving that authority validates the associates' worth and frees them to achieve. Manage results, not process. Let team members make decisions along the way.

Show Appreciation

Show me a person who doesn't like praise, and I'll show you a person who doesn't like anything! Verbalize your gratitude for a job well done. All people are motivated by the praise of others. Let that praise come from you. Send thank-you notes and encouraging e-mail or text messages. Be lavish with compliments. If a team member is valuable to you, let him or her know it. People are looking for a reason to work hard. Give it to them.

Recognize Successes

Public recognition is a great impetus for quality ministry. It not only affirms the effort of the worker but also encourages ministry bystanders to volunteer. Bottom line: People work harder when they know they're being both watched and appreciated. Recognize success and it will be repeated. Ignore a victory and it may not happen again.

Involve People in the Journey

The old model of leadership was top down. Mandates were shoved downward like paper pills. The new model of leadership is participation oriented.

It allows people to contribute to the ministry in both planning and implementation. When workers feel that they are involved, they buy in to the project and are more apt to volunteer their creative talents. "We have a decision to make, and I'd like your opinion." The team member who hears that statement will follow the new direction, whether it was his idea or not.

Challenge People

Encourage them to stretch. Help them to understand that some pain accompanies gain. But you must also let them know that they are making an eternal difference. Show them that the rigor has rewards.

Show Compassion

Romans 12:15 says, "Rejoice with those who rejoice, and weep with those who weep" (NKJV). Stay connected. Pray for the needs of your workers.

Let them know you really care about them, and let them know you care about their families as well. Compassion is a crucial leadership skill.

Do you want to lead people? Get out in front of them, inspire them to change, and point the way. People are drawn to a good leader. Be one, and they will follow.

PART 6

COMMUNICATION

I love a commodious room, a soft cushion, a handsome pulpit.
But where is my zeal if I do not trample all these
underfoot in order to save one more soul?

—JOHN WESLEY

There is no speech or language where their voice
is not heard. Their voice goes out into all the earth,
their words to the ends of the world.

—PSALM 19:3–4

66

ESSENTIAL
PREACHING SKILLS

A church's growth may rise or fall on the strengths of its pastor's preaching.

Like every other ministry skill, preaching needs your constant attention—and constant improvement. Both the messenger and the message must be fresh in order to meet the needs of your audience. Here are some areas of attention.

Aim for Anointing

Anointing is like the wind. You can't see it, but you can feel it. You can't touch it, but you can see its effects. Anointing is the gentle movement of the Holy Spirit through the eyes, lips, hands, feet, and heart of the preacher. It's more important than a perfectly crafted manuscript. It has more influence than a recitation of facts and philosophies. It moves men and woman to change their spiritual *attitude* as well as their spiritual *altitude*.

A preacher with a passion for spiritual power to proclaim scriptural truth is one who is making a difference in the Kingdom. People are drawn to fire. A pulpit ministry that is alive with truth, enthusiastically and carefully proclaimed, is one that will attract hungering hearts.

Make sure that prayer and the study of God's Word take precedence over managerial duties. In the care and keeping of the local church, there will be a hundred and one demands for the minutes of your day. But no duty is of greater importance than keeping your heart alive and your ministry fresh from daily meetings with the Master.

Take in as much as you give out—or you'll give out! It's easier to put your brain in neutral and watch TV or play a computer game than it is to read an inspiring book. But truth be told, a moment with a classic or contemporary preacher who is influencing lives is better than an hour or two with actors or technicians who are only simulating life.

Spend the last moments before you preach talking to the Lord rather than to others. Others may be around during your preparation time, however. You may enlist a prayer team that will lay hands on you and ask for God's anointing on your message before you go out to the platform. And even during the prelude, you can have an audience with God. Pray for God's power before you preach.

Take some time away from your office work and get alone with God. Seek His direction in your next sermon series. Bare your heart before Him and ask Him for His infilling. Determine not to preach or teach under your own power. Your congregation will notice the difference.

Stay Current

Effective preaching will demand that you keep up to date on hot topics. Using a reference to a current event in the introduction, body, or close of your sermon helps your audience see the importance of applying scriptural truth to their daily lives.

Newspaper or Internet columns, blogs, news magazines, and other media are full of contemporary topics and illustrations that can be used to link current events with the historical truths of the Bible. One word of caution regarding the Internet. Double- or triple-check any information you get there unless you are using a well-known, well-respected site. Getting news from second- or third-hand sources can yield inaccurate facts.

Focus on the Bible

Some of the fastest growing churches in the nation are those that emphasize expository preaching. Unchurched persons who become "churched" need Bible preaching. Topical preaching certainly has its place, but it is much more demanding over the long haul. Preaching through the Bible offers your congregation a steady and well-balanced spiritual diet. Book by book, chapter by chapter, verse by verse, there is a wealth of material in the gold mine of God's Word.

Work on Your Presentation

Preaching is a craft—a craft that demands craftsmanship. It takes work to construct and present an interesting sermon. But an interesting sermon results in an interested audience. Pay attention to the sermon itself.

Does It Have an Attention-Grabbing Introduction? Can the main points be easily remembered? Have you made "bridges" between the main points with illustrations or quotes? Have you appealed to the emotions of the audience? What do you want the audience to do or feel as a result of the sermon? Do you have an interesting and thought-provoking close?

Have You Added Doors and Windows? We are a story-driven people. The wandering thoughts of your audience can be captured in the web of a good story! But make sure it's truthful. Make sure it's credited to its rightful owner. Make sure it appeals to the emotions. Then, go ahead: Utilize the main preaching and teaching method of the Master!

Have You Included Humor? Appropriate, relevant, and thoughtful humor can be an effective tool for communicating biblical truth. Some of the most interesting speakers you know are known for their humorous stories. Learn from them. Notice their timing. Watch their actions and reactions. See how they use a pause as a method of communication. Notice that they refrain from putting down others. See that they are unafraid of using their own foibles as a foundation for their story.

Also notice that they link the silly to the serious. Humor is a great bridge to a more serious subject.

Does It Have a Strong Application? You may have touched all the preaching bases in your sermon presentation, but you haven't hit a home run until you've touched the heart of your listener. A recitation of biblical truth is important, but an application of that truth is even more important. Your application of Bible truths to the everyday life of the listener will have an everyday influence.

The application may be done with a PowerPoint summary. You may include a video clip. You may use a narrative. A personal testimony may be used to clinch it. The methods may vary from sermon to sermon and moment to moment. But the fact is your listeners must see personally how your Saturday or Sunday message will work in their hearts once they get back to work on Monday!

67

PREACHING FOR
LIFE CHANGE

You're the pastor of a growing church. The music is fantastic; there are a hundred kids in the youth group; giving increases every month; everybody loves your preaching; new people are coming nearly every week; and the most frequent comment you hear is this: "I love this church—it's so much fun!"

What's wrong with that picture?

Nothing! as long as it includes lives being changed by the transforming power of the gospel. The usual markers of success in ministry (attendance, giving, and morale) don't always indicate, and can actually mask the true symptom of, church health—spiritual growth. Our job involves more than helping organizations thrive. It includes helping people become more like Christ. Life change is at the heart of our calling.

Lead for life change. What needs do people in your congregation face? What do they need to pick up, put down, or cast off in order to be transformed into Christ's likeness? What changes of heart, mind, habit, or life do they need in order to be more fully devoted to Christ?

On Sunday, October 8, 1871, D. L. Moody preached a message on Pilate from Matthew 27:22. In his conclusion, Moody read Pilate's famous question, "What shall I do, then, with Jesus who is called Christ?" "Take this text home with you and turn it over in your minds," Moody told the congregation. "Next Sabbath we will come to Calvary and to the Cross, and we will decide what to do with Jesus of Nazareth."

It would never happen.

Before the congregation was dismissed, fire engines could be heard in the streets. The great Chicago fire had begun. Three hundred lives would be lost in that blaze. Moody would never meet that assembled crowd again. He considered the conclusion of that service to be the greatest mistake in his preaching career.

Don't repeat it. When you have the opportunity to call for a decision, take it. Never let a person leave your hearing without knowing what to do—and being called to do it! Here's how to turn a simple sermon into a life-changing invitation.

Pray before You Minister

Is it too obvious? Ministry can't succeed without prayer. It is the Holy Spirit, not the preacher or teacher who convicts hearts. Pray for your own honesty and conviction. Pray that God will prepare hearts to receive His truth. Pray that the Spirit of God will move the hearts and minds of people. Pray in the study. Pray on the platform. Pray in the classroom. Pray in the pulpit. Pray as you make your call for Christ.

Present the Gospel

You'd think presenting the gospel would be a given. But many sermons or lessons make no mention of the good news. And you can't issue an invitation if you have nothing to offer. Put salvation on the table. Talk straight about sin. Pull no punches about judgment. Make the blood of Christ your turning point, and issue a lavish invitation to grace. Make it plain; that's the preacher's job.

Let the Bible Talk

These days, all of us are scrambling to grab the attention of the video generation. Savvy preachers and teachers use PowerPoint, sound bytes, video clips, and drama to make quick impact. That's useful, but there's a danger that our preaching and teaching will have the same value as a radio single: nice to hear, easy to forget. Add impact to your message by letting God speak through His Word. Read from the Bible, not phrases or single sentences, but whole verses and even entire paragraphs. Tell people, "This is the Word of the Lord." Few people will be impressed by what you or I say. When Scripture speaks they'll listen.

Offer a Clear Choice

To make a decision there must be a choice. Offer an option, and make it plain. Will anyone go to heaven by "taking one step closer to Jesus"—whatever that means? Are men and women saved by acknowledging that they've made "mistakes"? Let people know that they must confess sin, turn from it, and receive God's forgiveness by faith in Jesus Christ. They cannot accept God's offer of salvation if they don't know what it is.

Preach for Decision

"What about you?" Some version of those words should be heard in every sermon or lesson. Every time you minister, especially if you are presenting a salvation message, you must call people to do something about what they've heard. Presenting the good news means confronting people with the need to make a decision—something they'll put off if you let them. Don't. Call for a verdict.

Wait for a Response

Moody's greatest mistake was to say, "Go home and think about this." Home is the place where bills and telephones, television sets and chores crowd our minds and distract our attention. While the people are here—right here, right now—call them to respond, and then allow the time to do it. You don't have to sing one more verse a dozen times, but you can patiently and lovingly offer the opportunity to respond. Eternal lives depend on those few moments of grace.

Pilate's question remains unanswered in millions of hearts; thousands are in your community, and some are even in your church. Will you present the question? Will you call for a decision?

68

EARNING AN AUDIENCE'S ATTENTION

There they sit. You can almost see the scorecard in their hands. Your audience members have driven a few blocks or a lot of miles just to hear what you are going to say.

Do I have your attention yet? Communication is all about getting the attention of your audience. It's like sending a carrier pigeon on a flight from the platform to the audience and hoping someone will catch it and unroll the message tied around its leg before the final prayer and the beeline to the restaurant.

But you have an advantage over the restaurant owner. You get to go first. You won't want to miss that train! You have a tiny piece of time on your hands that may make an eternal difference in someone's life. You'll want to know how to reach that audience member who has chosen you over the eggs Benedict—at least for now.

There are several keys to reaching an audience.

Act Natural

You may be as nervous as a snake crossing the interstate. But don't let it show. Breathe deeply. Take a lingering sip from your water bottle until the butterflies nest. Remember, these people came to hear you, not the pastor down the street. They're already yours!

Whatever you need to do in order to act natural, do it. But don't admit it!

Win Them Early

You only have a few minutes to "break the sound barrier." You only have a few minutes to win the attention of your audience. You won't want to drop the ball. Get their attention with a top-ten list, a funny story about getting ready for church, a shocking fact or figure; or make their eyes pop with an eye-popping quote from a celebrity. Once you've made the invisible leap from the platform into those rows of pews or chairs without falling on your face, you're almost home.

Look Them in the Eye

You already know what the ceiling looks like. Why look at it when you have such a lovely audience to gaze upon? Notice some of the most well-known public speakers. Watch their eyes. They're probably looking at you! Audience members want to be in on the message, not left out. You can read your notes once in awhile without preaching to them. Preach to your audience instead.

Make it personal. While you're speaking, start at the left of the auditorium and slowly scan to the right. Then, start at the right and take the reverse trip. When you've finished (and while you're still speaking) look to the back of the auditorium, and then look to the front (and, don't forget the balcony!). The slow but constant motion of your attention will be of great help in keeping your audience's attention.

Communicate at Their Level of Understanding

There's no use talking about the good ol' days to a twenty-something crowd. These *are* the good ol' days to them! And giving tips on text messaging Scriptures to an audience of senior saints will be a waste of your time and theirs. Think about the crowd. Think about their biblical literacy. Think about their interests. Think about their knowledge of theological terms. Communicate to them at a level that brings the "I get it!" look to their eyes.

Focus on the Friendly Few

There will be one or more in your audience who will be with you from your very first words. Don't forget them. You may need them later on. Those who seem to be getting every word you say—and liking those words—are your fans. They may be fickle enough to mark your scorecard low the next time around, but they're yours for this go-around. Come back and visit them during your message. After you've made your sight journey around the sanctuary, return to their friendly faces.

Appeal to the Senses

There's a reason people stand when the flag bearers march down the aisle of your auditorium. It's a feeling of patriotism. Your audience has feelings. They want to be happy and sad, sorrowful and joyful. Appeal to their senses. For example, take them to the Holy Land during your message on the temptation of Jesus. Let them "hear" the wind whistling around the mountain. Let them "feel" the sandy soil under His feet. Let them "see" the lonely look in the eyes of the Son of God during His attack by Satan.

Use words and phrases that will make your audience feel like they are personal witnesses to what you are speaking about.

Move Slowly

You can move around the platform without making it look like you are in a ballet. Move, but move slowly. A constant trip from one side of the platform to the other may do more to shorten the attention span than it will to widen it.

Use gestures. There's a reason we enjoyed doing the motions to those Sunday school songs. Movement made us feel like we were a part of the presentation. Practice using hand gestures while you are practicing your message in front of a mirror. I can just picture the sweeping motion of the Master's hand as He talked about the fields that were whitened to harvest. I can almost see Him reach out and touch the blinded eyes. Gestures are great tools for keeping the attention of your audience.

Adapt Quickly

As sure as the world, someone's cell phone is going to ring during one of your most important points. Don't panic. Use the incident to your advantage. Tie it to the point or illustration. That will make the audience feel at ease—and remind the cell phone user to use the "vibrate" setting.

God has given you eyes, ears, voice, lips, hands, and feet—and a brain and heart. Use them effectively and you'll never lack attention.

69

HOW TO GET YOUR MESSAGE ACROSS

Every week you face the challenge of communicating with your congregation. Babies cry, air conditioners rattle, children squirm, adults watch the clock. Does *anybody* hear the message?

Yes. They hear it, and they need it.

Never forget that it's by the "foolishness of preaching" that men and women are saved (1 Cor. 1:21 KJV). God ordained preaching as a means of spreading the gospel, and He ordained you to do the job.

Communication is never simple, but it's not an impossible task. Good communication demands constant evaluation, such as whether a connection has been made between the source (that's you) and the receiver (your audience). Here are some common problems in communication—and what to do about them!

Words

Words can actually hamper your communication effort—especially when you mispronounce them! If the Scripture passage you'll be reading aloud on Sunday morning includes names of biblical cities, countries, or people, familiarize yourself with the pronunciation before you speak.

Also, please don't say "nu-cu-lar" when you mean "nuclear." Don't say real-a-tor when you mean "realtor." And please avoid talking about John "Why-cliff" when you mean John Wycliffe (pronounced wih-cliff) or Frederick "Booch-ner" when you mean Frederick Buechner (pronounced beek-ner).You're an educated person and your audience undoubtedly includes well-read adults. You'll irritate your congregation unnecessarily by mispronouncing common words. And never, ever use a word (including slang) if you're not absolutely certain of its definition! You'll only embarrass yourself and your congregation.

Every generation develops its own vocabulary, and many disciplines have their own lingo. The church has its own "language" too. We use specialized terms such as sin, grace, eschatology, and atonement. And we have plenty of religious jargon, phrases like "personal Savior" and "get saved." Your hearers may come from a background where that language wasn't spoken. When you communicate, "translate" these terms for those who listen. Be certain you are using terms every listener can readily understand.

Attention Span

The average attention span for an adult is between nine and eleven minutes. But the average sermon is thirty minutes long! Though this is the same length as a television sitcom, remember that your listeners may "change channels" several times during that half hour. Give them something to listen for. Vary your pitch, rate, and volume. Use humor. Repeat. Help your listeners stay tuned.

Different Grids

People come from different backgrounds—social, ethnic, and educational. The audience's background directly affects its ability to listen and learn. Hearers will filter everything you say through the grid of their experience. That's why it is important to know your audience.

Understand who they are, where they've been, and where they are now. You can increase your impact by reducing the static of your message as it passes through the grid of your hearers.

Learn to speak the language. There are definite cultural understandings that can be incorporated in your message. Use them carefully and cautiously, but use them to make a bridge between you and your audience.

Baggage

Some of your Sunday morning attendees arrive with an armload of "spiritual Samsonite"—personal baggage that affects the way they listen. Many congregations have members who are socially dysfunctional and are either trying to work through these problems or are actively in denial. Reduce the effect of listener baggage by being attuned to visual cues from the audience. Read body language. Watch facial expressions. Evaluate the effect your words are having on the audience. If your message is not getting through, regroup mentally and take a different approach. Be like the quarterback who breaks the huddle, lines the offense up, and then reads the defense. He will often have to change plays—on the spot.

Information Overload

It's Sunday morning. People wake up listening to the radio, probably tuned to an "all bad news" station. They may continue by watching the news on television as they eat breakfast. They may even scan the newspaper or check their e-mail before leaving the house. In the car, they'll listen to the radio again. Once at church, they'll "prepare" for the service by reading the bulletin. By the time you preach, they will have ingested several hours worth of information from a variety of media.

But you can make yourself heard above the noise by communicating effectively. Master your message in the study so you will own it in the pulpit. Make personal contact with your hearers by eye contact, appropriate gestures, and movement. Above all, stick to the subject. Don't utter a single word that doesn't drive home the point of your message.

Skepticism

Audiences are more suspicious than they have ever been—and in many cases rightly so. Some listeners have been disillusioned or disappointed by public figures—including religious leaders. As a result, they're on the lookout for character and integrity flaws in those who communicate with them. Break through that tough exterior by being genuine. Be appropriately self-revealing when you preach. Avoid making yourself the hero of every story. Be honest about yourself without running yourself down. When the audience trusts you, it will listen to you.

Communication is always challenging, never more so than today. But preaching is still the most effective means of communicating the most important message to your congregation. Master these skills, and you will be heard!

70

USING STORY

IN PREACHING

Jesus spoke more truth in minutes than we will speak in a lifetime of communicating. But how did He drive the truth home? with a parable— a story. Master the art of storytelling and you will master the art of communicating. But not all stories are created equal. Some will have a snooze factor, and others will light mental or emotional fires that will burn forever.

If I were to use the phrase "It was the touch of the master's hand," what would come to mind? An auction? A low bid? A stringed instrument? A musician? The answer is all of the above. It is probably one of the most well-known stories ever preached. A violin is put up for bid at an auction. The violin wasn't exactly a Stradivarius in appearance. Time had dimmed its shine, its strings were loose, its chin rest was gone, and the auctioneer probably had to blow dust from the bout (body).

The auctioneer asked for bids. The bidding was pathetically low— only a dollar. Then a gentleman stood up from the audience and walked to the front of the room. Asking if he could play the violin, he put it under his chin, tightened the bow, adjusted the strings, and a beautiful melody flowed from it. You remember the outcome: The crowd cheered. And suddenly the bidding jumped from one dollar to one thousand. The difference is told in the punch line: "It was the touch of the master's hand."

The story bridges to a person's salvation. The heart without Christ seems worthless. But once Christ gets a hold of it, it increases in value. The story and its message have touched untold thousands of lives. What is there about a story that makes it a firelighter instead of a snoozer? I think there are at least eight characteristics of a good story or illustration.

It Is Biblical

You're a Christian communicator. You're locked in to this one! When you took that Bible into your hands at the ordination service, you pledged to preach it—in sermons and with accompanying illustrations. For you, a good story always ends up in Bible land with a definite tie to a scriptural truth.

It Is Believable

You've probably been to an auction. And you've probably bid low on an item. So have your listeners. If they haven't been to an auction personally, they've probably seen one on TV. They've watched as classic cars were pushed into the spotlight. They groaned at the low bids and gasped at the high.

Your story must relate to the experience of your audience. Would they understand the auction analogy? Why? If your story doesn't meet people at street level, they'll probably head for higher ground.

It Is Logical

A good story has a good beginning and a good ending. And the path from the introduction to the conclusion is plainly marked. How will you know that it is logical in its sequence? Tell it out loud. Better yet, tell it to a friend or family member. If one of those puzzled looks cloud their face and a question mark seems to appear over their head, you're in trouble!

It Is Practical

A good story doesn't just fill gaps between the "good mornings" and the "in conclusions." It has an obvious reason for being there. It will provoke thought. It will call for a decision. Hopefully, your story will affect people in such a way that they will want to know more about Christ—not just more about the story. It will make a spiritual impact. Audience members will gain from it.

How can you tell if the story will impact others? Did it affect you? Did it make you think, move, or increase your devotion to Christ? You've found a good story!

It Is Emotional

A good story appeals to the senses. Audience members won't just hear it, they will cry over it. Or they will take the journey from a chuckle to a belly laugh. They will grow nostalgic. They will envision the sights and sounds. You're not preaching to trees—though a few may look like they were cut from a petrified forest. They are very human people with very human emotions. Don't forget that!

It Is Valuable

Good stories have an "aha" factor. Audience members will want to remember them. They will write them on tithing envelopes. They will pass them along at their earliest convenience. They will hold them to their heart and treasure them forever.

It Is Transferable

A story without meaning isn't worth telling. A story is a bridge to biblical truth. A story is a vehicle that will take your audience to the destination of your message—and allow them to enjoy the trip. Think about that when you get ready to file it. Think about that when you put it into that "wonder" sermon. Think about that even as you are telling it. *How will this story bring me to the close of my point, or to the end of my sermon?*

Go ahead. You can do it! You may think you can't tell a good story, but you can. You told your friends and family about that vacation trip, didn't you? You described to an associate that ordeal of finding a parking spot at the mall on Christmas Eve. You drew a conclusion from those incidents and it made a difference in the mood of your listener. Just think of how your story may make a difference in the eternal dwelling of your listener!

71

USING HUMOR EFFECTIVELY

If your church members are watching *Saturday Night Live*, they won't settle for "Sunday Morning Dull." Humor is a great way to include your congregation in the service. Though pastors should never feel as if they are competing with late night TV, they are wise to learn how to intersperse humor in their sermon and teaching situations. The effective use of humor is just as important as its selective use.

Humor is a wonderful way to gain attention, put people at ease, hold their interest, and clarify truth. "Three points and a poem" may sail over the heads of the audience like a paper airplane made from a bulletin, but often a humorous story—linked to scriptural truth—will make its way to the heart of the listener and long be remembered.

There are several other important "humor laws" that can be applied to your presentation.

Law One: Use Humor Carefully

A humorous story told just for the sake of hearing laughter is empty and, perhaps, vain. Humor must have an ultimate purpose; it must be a bridge that links truth. The common expression applies here: "What's your point?" Ask yourself some important questions:

To whom am I speaking?

What is the most positive way to say it?

What is the most interesting way to say it?

Law Two: Use Humor Sensitively

A friend of mine was sitting on the platform waiting to preach to a large camp meeting audience. He took advantage of the preservice time to glance at his sermon notes one last time. Looking up from his notes to view the gathering crowd, he spotted an amputee with a hand prosthesis—metal clamps. Just as he noticed the amputee, he glanced again at his notes to discover that his opening "cute story" was about a man who looked like a pirate who had answered an ad for a sea captain. You guessed it! The applicant in the story had a hooked hand.

The story had to be abandoned immediately. But in the process, my friend began to think about similar stories that may cause discomfort to someone at the expense of a fast laugh.

Law Three: Use Humor Skillfully

A forgotten punch line, a failure to include pertinent story details, or a failure to speak distinctly can result in a pregnant pause that gives birth to an embarrassing moment of silence. Humor has several integral elements. It must be relevant, have an obvious punch line, be well timed, be concise, and have a payoff.

Law Four: Use Humor Occasionally

A steady line of stories, one-liners, or jokes shouldn't be used as a substitute for careful teaching and preaching of biblical principles. They should be used occasionally. The speaker who tries to compete with the comedy channel will find himself subject to the mental "remote control" of the audience.

Law Five: Use Humor Effectively

The speaker should study the experts. What is conspicuous about their delivery? Timing? Eye contact? Material? Reaction to "bombs"? Learn from the pros. But learn without obviously copying their mannerisms. Learn to be original. Humor should be an offspring of your own personality.

Law Six: Use Humor Selectively

Humor must fit the demographics of the audience. A story about living in downtown Los Angeles, for instance, will be met with significant silence if it's told to an audience in a Nebraska farming community.

Law Seven: Use Humor Respectfully

Spouses and family members are often a good source of humor. Everyday incidents in the home are often hilarious. But restraint should be used, and permission granted, before those personal stories are used in a public arena. It would be better to make yourself the "fall guy" rather than a family member.

Law Eight: Use Humor Wisely

Often, a personal story with a humorous slant or a careful comment about some "absurd" current event will have a greater impact than a well-rehearsed joke.

There are several factors that bear consideration in the delivery of humor:

Attitude. Do you feel good about the story? If it doesn't make sense to you and if you don't feel good about it, it probably will be received like an ugly cousin's kiss.

Rehearsal. You will be more comfortable if you rehearse your humorous stories. Often you can try out a humorous story on your family or friends. If that story is met with stone-cold silence, it probably will have the same impact in church!

Timing. Often a pause is as good as a punch line. Probably no other comedian mastered the pause better than TV host Johnny Carson. Long after you have forgotten his stories, jokes, or one-liners, you'll remember his long pause and the lingering look to the audience.

Motion. Both your location and your gestures can be used to keep your audience alert. In using a humorous opening story, you may want to consider moving away from the stage or platform, perhaps walking toward the audience. By moving from your "comfort zone" to the "battle zone" you may disarm your audience and make them alert.

Careful hand gestures also add to your humorous story. Like the hand motions of children's Sunday school songs, "doing the motions" of a story will help you communicate it.

Eye Contact. One confidence builder is to spot the person who best reacts to your humor and deliver the punch line directly to her or him. And if you're in luck, your mother will be in the crowd!

Good Taste. You've probably heard your parents say, "We don't talk about those things in public." That's still good advice. There are some topics that are definitely off-limits in your presentation. For example, humor that deals with bodily functions is always in bad taste. Likewise, humor about an alternate lifestyle or one with a racial overtone is out of place in the pulpit. Humor is used in the healing process, not the hurting process.

I once read that everyone needs a funny bone as well as a backbone. Appeal to both and you will improve your communication skills.

72

HOW TO TALK
ABOUT MONEY

T alking about money can be as hazardous as using a chain saw—
and just as dangerous. Often people like to talk about money
anywhere but in the church. You spend six weeks preaching
about wise stewardship and most of the time, your congregation will
either have the look of a deer in headlights or look like they've just
overdosed on cold medicine.

Hurdling over the money barrier is necessary to a whole-life ministry.
You *can* talk about money. But what you say and how you say it will often
make a difference in red or black numbers on the treasurer's financial
statement—and sometimes in the tenure of your ministry.

The first thing to consider is that talking about money isn't just talking
about *money*. Giving is not just about receipts; it is about reactions to
the mission of your church or organization. You must be clear about the
fact that money is simply a tool for ministry. It is a vital part of your
church's mission. You will do a disservice to your people when you talk
more about finances than mission.

Some of you are facing ministry challenges right now. You need
more money, more volunteers—more people to step up with their time,

talent, and treasure. What you need is a spirit of giving. That's what happens when a congregation becomes a giving church!

Granted, money is one of the subjects every preacher tiptoes around. It seems there's no way to win. When you ignore it, people conclude that stewardship is unimportant. When you preach or teach about it, you hear the age-old complaint: "All the church wants is my money!"

Here are some tips for talking about finances that leave people happy to give.

Don't Be Afraid of It

Speaking about finances can be intimidating for a pastor. After all, we're preachers, not pundits. If we were financial wizards, we'd be on Wall Street, not in the pulpit. But the Bible talks about money a lot. It was one of Jesus' favorite subjects, and both Peter and Paul had pointed words for believers on this topic. The man or woman of God has full authority to speak about finances from a biblical and spiritual perspective. You need not be a certified financial planner to teach stewardship. If we're silent on this important subject, we validate the selfish use of money that pervades our culture. Teach tithing!

Connect It to Ministry

God wants more than our money (it's really His anyway). He wants our whole life. Help your people see that giving money is only one-third of the stewardship equation. Time and talent make up the rest. Checkbook charity is not biblical. Every Christian needs to exercise his or her spiritual gift(s) along with donating money. Teach a balanced view of stewardship.

Teach Opportunity over Obligation

Some Christians think of giving to God's work as an obligation—something we're stuck with. How sad! Contributing to its mission is one of the greatest privileges of being in the church. Saint Augustine said,

"Where your pleasure is, there is your treasure. Where your treasure is, there is your heart. Where your heart is, there is your happiness."

Giving toward the church's worldwide ministry can be a great motivator. Your stewardship message may include something like this: "God is moving on the mission field. The overseas church is adding thousands of new believers each day. We're a vital part of that when we support missionaries!"

There are tremendous needs in your community. Tying the opportunity of giving to a local need may also be a great motivator. Ask, "How many unchurched families live within five miles of our church? How many children? Think of the possibilities! What might God do if we would be willing to give our time, talent, and treasure to meet the needs of people in our local community?"

You must emphasize that tithing is an opportunity to see God work, never an obligation.

Let Others Speak

The pastor's voice should not be the only one heard on the subject of money. In fact, the more people who are involved in the teaching, the more effective it will be.

Invite individuals or families who tithe to share their testimonies. You'll be amazed to hear how God has blessed them through this simple act of faith—and so will your people! Real stories will inspire real people to trust God by tithing.

Invite a Christian accountant or financial planner to speak about stewardship. Working in the business world gives such a person a unique perspective. He or she will draw a sharp contrast between the greedy attitude of the world and the contented attitude of the Christian regarding money. This "professional opinion" will add weight to your teaching.

Model Your Teaching

A word of caution: Don't teach tithing if you don't tithe. You must be prepared to practice what you preach on this issue. Money and sex are the two areas where the world most hates hypocrisy. Model your financial teaching in your own life. You may want to be the very first person to put a check or tithing envelope in the offering plate during the worship service.

Show the congregation that church finances are handled according to biblical principles. Pay your denominational assessment in full and on time. Place Kingdom needs before congregational comfort. And treat the church's income like what it is: God's money on loan to God's people for doing His work.

Celebrate Successes

Did you pay off the mortgage? Have a party! Did you reach your annual goal for missions giving? Let people know! When your church reaches a financial milestone, no matter how small, call attention to it. You will reinforce the truth of your teaching. Handling money God's way really works!

Play the Faith Card

The use of money is a spiritual indicator. Make sure your people understand that. Hoarding money shows that we don't trust God. Wasting money shows that we don't respect Him. Greed, covetousness, materialism, miserliness, stinginess—these behaviors offer a window into the soul.

Connecting successful projects to faithful giving is an important lesson in stewardship. "This new building (or carpet, or van, or remodeling project) is an example of your faithfulness in giving your time, talent, and treasure to the Lord. God helped us do this because you were obedient in giving."

Help your people make the connection between the heart and the bank statement. Jesus did.

73

COMMUNICATING YOUR VISION IN WRITING

When you turned in that paper on expository preaching to your college professor, you thought your writing days were over. Little did you know that it was only the first step in a lifelong journey of words, sentences, paragraphs, and punctuation marks. It wouldn't be just sermon manuscript writing. It would be writing bulletin announcements, newsletters, online columns, news releases, letters of recommendation, letters to the editor, *ad infinitum.* Just listing your writing "opportunities" is enough to make you weary.

But the benefits are thrilling. My writing, in addition to my preaching and teaching, has taken me to places I never imagined when I wrote my first term paper. In fact, I wondered if I would ever see the light outside the classroom. Overseas seminars and conferences that feature one of my books have given me a host of new experiences—and a wealth of new friendships.

Where will you begin your writing journey? Begin where I did: with an idea and an empty page. And then get ready for the rest of the trip. Getting from the idea to the page takes a plan—a writing journey. Let me share a few thoughtful stops along the way—in the form of some basic writing concepts.

Determine Your Destination

What is your writing mission? Why are you writing the article or book? For fame and fortune? (Sorry, Christian writing has very little of that.) To set people straight? (Not a God-pleasing motivation.) Or, to use your talents to help others in their spiritual journey? The latter is best. Imagine your writing as an extension of your ministry.

The apostles were on a mission. But they couldn't take their mission to more than one church at a time. That's why they burned the midnight oil in transferring their thoughts to parchment. Their writings would take them to places they could never otherwise reach. Focus on your mission.

Identify Your Fellow Travelers

Who Are Your Readers? Your writing must fit the demographic of the audience. An article about eight-track audio tapes, for instance, will be met with cold stares if it's written to teenagers more familiar with digital video discs (DVD) and MP3 audio technology. Write to the audience's level of understanding.

What Do Your Readers Need? They need biblical truth. They need to learn how to get from point A to point B without falling prey to the enemy of their faith. They need some prodding, as well as some encouraging. Finley Peter Dunne, one of the great journalists of the 1900s, wrote that a writer's job is to "comfort the afflicted and to afflict the comfortable." Which do your readers need right now?

What Will Your Reader Need Later On? Write with their future in mind. Writing crosses time zones. Listen for the future. On a clear night, you can hear a train coming from far away. The sound is faint at first, but a careful listener can hear it. Writers listen for the train that has not yet arrived. They look for trends that are just over the horizon.

Map Your Writing Journey

There is no mystery to the preparation of a good article or book. As with building a house, there are stages of construction. The builder who follows a plan and stays on schedule will produce a sound structure. You'll also need a map for your writing journey.

What Will Be Your First Point of Interest? Whether writing for profit or writing to inform or inspire your own parishioners, the lead, or first few paragraphs of an article, must grab the reader. Without a strong beginning, your reader will be turning the magazine page for something more interesting.

Abraham Maslov noted that people desire safety, security, a sense of belonging, and to make a difference in their world. Engage them on the feeling level: "Do you ever feel alone in a church of two thousand?" "Is your prayer life stale and boring?"

Or simply start with a story or a quote, but make sure you can verify its authenticity with at least two sources. (Using urban legends discredits you as an author.) A humorous anecdote is also an effective lead.

How Will You Keep Your Readers with You? Reader incentives are found in quotations, humorous or inspiring stories, and other material that adds interest to your subject. A wise writer is constantly on the lookout for illustrations. Scan the newspaper. Subscribe to good magazines. Notice what's popular on television and in film. Jot down observations. Surf the Net. Keep the interest of the reader in mind, and then keep on the lookout for interesting material.

Where Will You Get Your Supplies for the Journey? Speaking of interesting materials, when you find good material, where will you keep it? Good supplies, like good writing materials, are stored for safety. When you find good material, file it. Be good to your files, and they'll be good to you. You'll need that illustration or story some day.

Ask for Directions

You've just begun your journey. Others are familiar with the writing terrain. Editors, like wilderness guides, can keep you on track and help you see the dangerous spots. Ask a friend to read your piece—critically. Join a writers' critique group (you can find groups by contacting your local library). And remember, the secret to good writing is rewriting!

Rely on the Holy Spirit

The Bible promises the guidance of the Holy Spirit in discovering truth. If you will be effective in your writing, your co-writer must be God's Spirit. He has not only promised to show you the way; He has promised to empower you *along* the way. God will use your words and sentences to enlighten, inspire, and edify your readers.

So start writing, and have a good journey!

74

Keys to a Successful Board Meeting

Ministry often includes the boredom of boards and a commitment to committees. Meetings consume much of the energy of a leader. One administrative goal may be to take the boredom out of board meetings and put the commit into committee meetings. It doesn't happen accidentally. It is planned—and carried out. There is a reason board or committee members leave those meetings with the satisfaction of accomplishment. Let's look at some ingredients for a successful meeting—a meeting that accomplishes its purpose and gathers the team in a quest for excellence.

Preparation

The Bible is a book of preparation. The Old Testament sets the agenda, and the New Testament turns it into accomplishments. Jeremiah 29:11 reads, "'For I know the plans I have for you,' declares the LORD, 'plans to prosper you and not to harm you, plans to give you hope and a future.'" Christian leaders are called to carry out God's plans. And they do it through people who are organized around the mission.

Simply calling a meeting doesn't ensure its success. Successful meetings are planned. They have a purpose.

Meetings need direction. People who have made commitments of their time and energy should know the reason why. At the beginning of the board or committee appointment, you might distribute a mission, purpose, and job description to make sure everyone on the board or committee knows what is expected.

Organization

Jesus advised planning. "Suppose one of you wants to build a tower. Will he not first sit down and estimate the cost to see if he has enough money to complete it?" (Luke 14:28). Organization for your meeting may include:

The Agenda. The agenda is the road map for your meeting. Like a computerized map calculation, it shows you where you are, where you are going, and estimates how long it should take you to get there. The agenda is important for a couple of reasons. First, it keeps the meeting on track. It is always dangerous to open the meeting for suggestions on items to be covered. Often participants will sidetrack the meeting and end up in unnecessary—and often heated—conflict. Second, it keeps you from all-nighters. A meeting without an agenda is open to endless discussion about unimportant issues.

Room Preparation. The comfort of the participants adds to the quality of the meeting—and communicates organization. Room temperature should be adjusted; refreshments might be prepared; the meeting table is cleaned and supplied with pen and paper; the agenda is placed at every seat; and multimedia equipment has been tested.

Minutes. A recording secretary should be appointed for every meeting. The main actions (not the entire discussion) should be noted, summarized, spell-checked, and distributed at the following meeting. Proper minutes of the meeting help to deter the "he-said-she-said" of follow-up meetings.

Devotions. Yours is a Christian meeting. God's Word should be honored by its reading, and prayer should be offered for God's will to be accomplished through the participants. The devotional time also gives an opportunity for others to communicate. If the chairperson always gives devotions, participants won't be able to share in the ownership of the meeting.

Wrap-Up. Summarizing the actions of the board meeting does two things: First, it gives the participants a sense of accomplishment; second, it gives an opportunity for the chairperson to end the meeting. "This has been a good meeting." "We have accomplished . . ." "Our next meeting is scheduled for . . ."

Communication

The chairperson's responsibility is to communicate—orally or in print—the information necessary for the meeting participants to make decisions about the agenda items and receive reports.

Expression

Successful meetings include the opportunity for the members to have their say. Church-related meetings should be an exercise in democracy. The participants not only present their own ideas and ideals, they represent those whom they represent. Open communication acknowledges freedom of speech, no matter how rambling the comments.

Compassion

The hidden agenda in every meeting agenda is the spiritual, social, and financial welfare of the members. Behind every message, meeting, and action of the Savior was the underlying purpose of seeking and saving the lost. Hearts that are warmed by the fire of the Holy Spirit will show compassion to the needs of the entire organization. A compassion-driven meeting is always a successful meeting—no matter what action was or wasn't taken.

The church should take the lead in compassionate ministries. That compassion can be expressed in planning or in giving, in organizing or in building. What you accomplish through a board or committee must have Kingdom building as its primary goal.

Church organizational meetings can be a wonderful way for people to grow in their faith, in their service to others, and in realizing their spiritual gifts. They can be times of inspiration, times of vision, and times of just plain fun. But they should always be a time of sincere communication about ministry happenings.

Don't forget, it was a committee of twelve who was given the job of spreading the gospel to the entire planet!

75

STAYING ON
THE CUTTING EDGE

With today's rapid changes in technology, it's easy to get left behind. Christian leaders can keep ahead of the game by staying informed. In the information age, knowledge is power. Here's how to keep yourself on the cutting edge.

Read Constantly

All of us in ministry have ready access to the information we need to enhance our spiritual growth, to strengthen the spiritual growth of our parishioners, and to heighten the spiritual and organizational growth of our church or organization. Christian leaders must be learners—and learners are readers.

Finding time to grow in your knowledge of ministry methods to a postmodern world can be challenging. The very nature of that world is immediacy: Do it now! Buy it now! Learn it now! The problem with that is that every part of your ministry is in the now. Daily demands put a burden on contemporary ministers that is perhaps the greatest in history.

Once a mark on a calendar was enough to keep your schedule under control. Now, it takes the calendar plus a desktop, laptop, or hand-held computer to get us to where we need to be in time to do what needs to be done. Factoring reading time into a day that is already too long will be a struggle.

Thankfully, it can be done. You can be on the cutting edge of knowledge regarding your ministry. How?

- Peruse online news services.
- Subscribe to trade magazines and journals.
- Read news magazines and even blogs.
- Keep a good book on your nightstand (and open it once in awhile!).
- Make the most of your time by learning to pick the meat from an article or news item and leave the bones. Prioritize your reading as you do your other tasks.

Learn on the Move

Being wired isn't a luxury for a twenty-first-century Christian leader; it is a necessity. Keeping current means having mobile sources of information. Yesterday's cutting-edge leaders listened to cassette tapes on long car rides. Today's leaders get Podcasts of the latest information in their field. In both cases the principle is the same—make good use of your time by never being out of touch.

Most pastors, for instance, spend hours on the road. The most important use of that drive-time is spent in prayer—for family, for parishioners, for national leaders, for denominational leaders, and for shut-ins. The second most important use of drive-time is learning. Christian ministry is constantly changing. New technology mixed with new methods—that tell the same trusted message—is continually stretching the knowledge and experience of the minister.

Utilize the Internet

Surfing the Net can be as dangerous as surfing the highest waves of a shark-infested ocean. Building in personal safeguards while taking advantage of the wealth of resources on the Internet is challenging at best. But the billions of Internet pages include the good along with the bad. Christian Web sites offer resources that once took a roomful of books on bookshelves. Online searches get you to those resources faster than a team of librarians. Bible translations, commentaries, dictionaries, quotation books, illustrations, and style manuals are literally at your fingertips. Plus, you can gain almost instant knowledge of current events through news networks online.

That illustration for the weekend sermon is only a click away. That piece of equipment for the nursery is available online at discounted prices. That technology that will turn Boomers and Busters from mere observers into believers is right there.

Seminars and teachings from the experts on church ministry can be downloaded and listened to at your convenience. Never before has the Christian ministry had such available tools for building the Kingdom. Use the technology, but don't abuse it—or let it abuse you. God is doing a new thing, in a new way. He is allowing us to spread the gospel at warp speed, and letting us learn how to use trusted methods for preaching, teaching, and broadcasting His timeless truth.

Network

The best leaders do not hoard information, and good leaders typically learn from each other. In your building, in your city, and within your field of specialty, there are opportunities to pick the brain of other leaders. Have coffee with the trendsetter in your ministerial association. Start a lunch roundtable with other clergy in your community. Tune into webinars or simulcasts that feature cutting edge information for your ministry. Learn from the best.

Benjamin Disraeli said, "As a general rule, the most successful man in life is the man who has the best information." He might have been speaking about the twenty-first century. In the information age, leaders have two choices: Get current or get left behind. Knowledge is power, and the leader who has the most usually wins.

But knowledge without power is pointless and dangerous. Cutting-edge ministry demands cutting-edge spirituality. God has always promised to get His message to the masses through very human people—often people without the opportunity for advanced learning. But learning without a vibrant love for Christ serves little more than self-promotion. Again, the Apostle Paul offers important advice: "For Christ did not send me to baptize, but to preach the gospel—not with words of human wisdom, lest the cross of Christ be emptied of its power" (1 Cor. 1:17).

What is the next thing you will do to keep yourself not just current with, but out in front of, the knowledge revolution?

AFTERWORD

After more than thirty years in pastoral ministry, I'm more excited than ever about building God's kingdom through the local church. What a privilege! I've shared with you a number of the lessons I've learned along the way, and I hope you've found them helpful. We're learning together.

Yet I realize that this book cannot address every situation you may face. No book can—there is too much to learn, and our world is constantly changing. As pastors, we need ongoing training, support, and encouragement. One of the most valuable tactics that I've found for continuing my growth is to build networks with other pastors. I invite you to join me by visiting www.stantoler.com, where you'll find lots of ministry resources including *Stan Toler's Leadership Newsletter*, my monthly electronic communiqué for pastors and church leaders.

Still have questions about ministry? Every month I answer pastors' questions about real life and real ministry. Look for the free Q & A online and submit your own question.

Pastor, you are engaged in the highest of all callings: service to the Lord Jesus Christ. Be encouraged! We're serving a Kingdom that cannot fail! Let's serve with joy and boldness—until He comes.

STAN TOLER
www.stantoler.com